*sister*
# SOLACE

RITUALS OF LOSS AND DESIRE

Mary Sojourner

SCRIBNER

NEW YORK   LONDON   TORONTO   SYDNEY

SCRIBNER
1230 Avenue of the Americas
New York, NY 10020

For information about special discounts for bulk purchases,
please contact Simon & Schuster Special Sales:
1-800-456-6798 or business@simonandschuster.com.

*Designed by Kyoko Watanabe*
Text set in New Baskerville

Manufactured in the United States of America

1   3   5   7   9   10   8   6   4   2

Library of Congress Cataloging-in-Publication Data
Sojourner, Mary.
Solace: rituals of loss and desire/Mary Sojourner.
p. cm.
1. Sojourner, Mary.
2. Authors, American—20th century—Biography.
3. Environmentalists—United States—Biography.
I. Title.

PS3569.O45Z47 2004
818'.5409—dc22
[B]

2003061020

ISBN 0-7432-2968-1

*In gratitude*
*to Lillian Chestney,*
*Susan Reynolds,*
*Susan Tasaki, she knows why,*
*to Mark Gant and his river-heart,*
*to Everett, a stand-up guy*
*who can take a trimmin'*

For the furthering of all sentient beings
and the protection of earth, air, and water.

*—a prayer that emerged September 25, 2001,*
*a few miles south of our sacred mountains*

# CONTENTS

■ ■ ■

## WHAT GOES AROUND COMES AROUND

What Goes Around Comes Around      3


## SCHEHERAZADE:
## A WOMAN TELLS STORIES TO SAVE HER LIFE

Scheherazade      9

Red Canoe      17

The Morning in the Heart of the Dark      20

Soul-Kissing in Purgatory      23

Kidnapped      27


## USING

Smoke: Visible Vapor Given Off by a
   Smoldering Substance      33

The Windows in the Gypsy Wagon Are
   Sheets of Mica      35

God Is Coming and She Is Pissed 41

Chief of Police Nixes Naked New Yorkers 44

The Myth of the Vaginal Orgasm 47

Fast-Forward 51

Brother Blood/Sister Solitude 57

Burning 61

## HUNTING SHELTER, FINDING SANCTUARY

Hunting Shelter, Finding Sanctuary 65

How to Leave: Leave 71

I'm Scared. I'll Do It. 74

Heading Home 78

Big Window 82

Animal Time 87

Dead Bill 89

Minimum Wage 94

## CRACK IN THE WORLD

Ev 101

Deathwatch 105

Crack in the World 111

Razor Vision 117

Now Somebody Else Knows     118

What Comes Around Goes Around     125


## DRASTIC MEASURES

What Catches You When You Stop Running     129

What the Simplicity Gurus Leave Out     135

Never Leave Your Machine     141


## MEDICINE

Doing Nothing     153

Daily     157

Occupying Less     160

The Essential     163


## SPIRIT LINE

Road Time     171

Spirit Line     180

Gratitude     189

*Acknowledgments*     191

# SOLACE

# WHAT GOES AROUND
# COMES AROUND

# What Goes Around Comes Around

■ ■ ■

I write to you from an eight-by-eight-foot weather-battered deck at the back of a little scrap-and-wallboard cabin near Flagstaff, Arizona. I would have come to this work sooner, but the dishwater began to boil on the woodstove—when you live in a home with no running water, you wash dishes when the water's hot.

It takes forty-five minutes to wash three days' worth of a single woman's dishes. And only four gallons of water, which, in a land whose rains are both ferocious and skittish, whose aquifers are being drained by development, gives me great joy. As does the half hour of carrying water from the shower house, plunging my hands into warm suds, and seeing the mismatched plates and glasses shine in the rack.

Now I sit in perfect sun. Long blue shadows weave across what's left of snow in the little meadow just beyond the two-trunked pine. It is mid-January, just past noon, at 6,900 feet. Cats wander through golden wild grasses. Harold, the tabby Forrest Gump; Buster, the hapless cat union organizer; Bluto, a suave Felix who moves like Jackie Gleason; the divine and terrible Miss ChiChi, her disposition and her sapphire eyes those of a forties movie empress.

I have come to what sometimes feels like paradise, other times like a difficult and inarguable exile, through no longer belonging anywhere else. I've moved through a hundred doors of dislocation—most often in pain, hanging on for what I believed was my dear life. Rarely, but joyfully, I've gone into surrenders so deep they felt like pure love.

Through all of this, there were no snipers. No one bombed my town. No one burned down my home. My children were not killed. We had more than enough to eat. More than enough of everything. I was one lucky American.

Now, luckier still, I know this red earth under my feet and the sweet light around me are gifts of shelter. And the work it takes to live here, a spiritual practice.

If you happened to look over from the old suburb a few hundred yards south of my back deck, you would see me, a sturdy woman, a Baba Yaga in black tights and hiking boots, perhaps the grown-up your parents warned you about. Or you might see a woman in part, or very much, like yourself. This woman will be writing.

*That* you can count on.

In twelve days, if I am lucky, I will be sixty-three. For fifty-two years of this life, I have written—sometimes randomly, sometimes more faithfully than I ever kept a lover. Poems. Stories. Essays. And journals. My daughter and my second best friend know they are to burn the journals when I die because the words in their pages are inseparable from my spirit. They are part of an intimate conversation with What I Serve. They are medicine. They are my best friend.

Earth and writing. I am held by them. They have carried me safely from my family, from serving as a mother, from the hope of connection with a partner toward a life in which I serve *them*. Earth and writing. My homes in human wilderness. My gratitude to them has become reason to live.

◆ ◆ ◆

The morning sun has moved behind the tall pines. The shadows are cobalt. I go back into the cabin. Juniper burns in the woodstove. Light pours through the big southern windows. There is no television, no washer, no dryer. There is an answering machine and fax. I have lived here sixteen out of the eighteen years I have been in the West. Not from noble environmental beliefs, but because this home in this plateau clearing is the first place I felt I truly belonged. The first home in which I could freely draw breath. The home in which I daily renew my vows to write and to fight for the earth.

I am a deeply devout woman. I pray with words, but more often with actions: picking up garbage from the forest roadside, dancing alone to the blues, using every drop of water I bring into my cabin, writing the ugly and essential, cutting up my big-box discount club card, being arrested while trying to stop a uranium mine from being sunk in a meadow known by a local tribe as the Belly of Mother Earth.

And I pray with inaction: Doing nothing. Faking patience. Keeping silence. Letting the next second, minute, hour unfold, in its own hard, its own sweet time.

Often, far too often, my prayers have been the muttering of a woman in passionate monologue with a man—or a slot machine—"Come on, baby. Give it up. You can do it."

I pray with a multitude of holy beings: the emerging dawn; Pan and the grasshopper nestled in his beard; the sound of ravens in flight—the *husshhh* of living feather on living wind; August thunder; the anger that flashes in my blood.

I serve the Goddess of the West, Our Lady of What Goes Around Comes Around. She informs every word, every silence in my work. She knows I stand firmly in the lineage of the obsessed, in the company of all who are hooked on anything we like. She asks me to live in this moment.

And in the long run.

# SCHEHERAZADE:
## A WOMAN TELLS STORIES TO
## SAVE HER LIFE

■ ■ ■ ■ ■ ■ ■ ■ ■ ■ ■ ■ ■ ■ ■ ■ ■

# Scheherazade

■ ■ ■

I warn you, I am an addict, a woman obsessed—by anything I like. Cilantro. Good gin. Smart men with black hair. E-mail. Slot machines whose wild symbol is a sloe-eyed Cleopatra. Adrenaline and the tsunami of beta-endorphins that follows terror.

A woman obsessed is rarely bored. And she is difficult. She needs patient friends, solitude, a talent for something. But more than anything, she needs a place to slow down, to stop, to take a breath. She needs shelter.

My brilliant mother suffered "nervous breakdowns." They were episodic and cyclical. They plunged her into psychosis, into terror so great she believed death to be the only release. She never succeeded in her suicide attempts, though not for lack of trying. The psychiatrists of those days could not help, nor could my overwhelmed and baffled father.

There were no reliable adults in my world, certainly no confidantes who could be trusted not to take my terror as accusation, no religious counselor who assured anything but punishment. In that world, books became shelter, stories my lifelines. I was in training. Unwitting. Going to words as root to soil.

*The girl is in her parents' bed. Her coloring books lie around her. She has a fever, perhaps not. Sometimes she is kept home from kindergarten to give her mother company. She hears her mother singing in the kitchen. The voice seems to waver, the words make no sense. She knows the singer is her mother. And is not. Her mother has been changing. Like a queen under an evil spell. It is better when her father is home, but he is at work. Her mother is not her mother. Her home is not her home. She wishes she could fall asleep and wake up when everything is safe.*

*She hears footsteps coming from the kitchen, coming toward her. There is nowhere to run, and she knows she must escape. She picks up a coloring book and pretends to read.*

*What happens next she will never remember. Except this: Mother is shelter, and a mother who is no longer a mother is a threat.*

*What she has learned to do she will never forget: how to disconnect.*

I came into reliable shelter first in October 1946—though now it seems as though *it* came to me. I was a sturdy six-year-old with fierce hazel eyes, sitting in a circle of other children in Miss Adams's reading class in Reuben Dake Grade School in Irondequoit, New York—a child brutally in need of haven, a home in which a mother did not shape-shift, and a father was a grown-up who would hold me close and whisper, "You're safe. I won't change."

What came to me in that first-grade reading circle was better. A little boy read aloud, stumbling through: See . . . Jane. See . . . Dick. See . . . Spot. Suddenly, his voice seemed to fade. I watched the words on the page in front of me begin to connect. See Jane. See Dick. See Spot. See Jane run see Dick run see Spot run—as if the words came alive and raced down the sidewalk between the grassy lawns of Jane and Dick's tidy neighborhood.

I checked to see if Miss Adams was watching. We weren't allowed to skip ahead. She was focused on the boy next to me. Stealthily, I turned the page. Jane and Dick and Spot were running down a long green hill toward a bright lake.

"Mary Elizabeth," Miss Adams said, "it is your turn." I looked up. She smiled. In that instant, I saw the bookshelves lining the classroom wall, and I knew I was not alone. I have a place to be safe, I thought, I won't ever be scared again. Ever.

*Here is a living room of a small apartment in early January of 1947. An Xmas tree glitters in the corner. The mother sits on the sofa. She pats the cushion next to her. The girl knows she is to sit down. "Can you see me shaking?" the mother whispers. "Can you?"*

*"No," the girl says, "you're not shaking. You're okay." The girl looks at the Xmas tree. She hopes the colors will help. She is not really crying, but when she squints, the lights explode, are colored stars, red, green, pure white as the possibility of real angels. She goes toward them, toward the possibility of losing herself.*

*And finds herself calm. Knowing there is more than one way to go away.*

When I was eight, my beloved grandfather Bill Foltz took me into his den. Bookshelves filled one wall. We sat on the floor and he pulled a thick leather-bound Bible from the bottom row. "There are stories here," he said, then waved at the shelves, "and here, and here."

I opened the Bible. It seemed alien. My father was Catholic and I was Catholic, and the Bible wasn't for Catholics. The pages of this Bible were crowded with spidery black-and-white drawings of sinking ships and lightning, empty deserts and clouds of fire. They scared me. I closed the book.

My grandfather smiled and took down another book. "Jules Verne," he said, *"Twenty Thousand Leagues Under the Sea."* He put the book in my hands and left. I read. Slowly. Carefully. It took nearly all summer, while my father was in graduate school and my mother, afraid to be alone, had brought us here to her father's house.

I don't remember much about Verne's world beneath the sea, but I do remember how, in the thick, wet heat of an Eastern summer, my grandfather's den was always cool; and no books were forbidden to me; and on the day my father came to take my mother and me home, my grandfather opened the old roll-top desk, handed me a freshly sharpened pencil and a blank pad, and said, "I don't have to tell you what these are for."

I won the local library's summer reading contest when I was ten. By three thousand miles. The librarians had posted a big map of America on the bulletin board. Each kid was given a paper car. For each book I read, I was allowed to advance the car fifty miles west. The prize was beyond price: the librarian would take the winner to a downtown bookstore to buy any book she wanted. By the end of the summer, I had gone across country three times and found my passion for the Road West—and for winning.

*The hallway is dark. The door is locked. The girl knows her mother and baby brother are in the apartment. And she knows her mother is again changed. She has no way to reach her father. He is at work and she has never been given the phone number.*

*There are grown-ups in the hardware store below the apartment. But the first rule is:* You never tell.

*She goes carefully down the stairs and sits on the bottom step. The light outside softens, goes cool. She imagines the light holds her safe. She takes a comic from her bookbag. She tells herself this story: all she has to do is read till the light is gone and her father will be home.*

In those days, comic books were for boys. Except for Archie and the Gang, and those were boring. I loved Red Ryder. He was a redheaded cowboy with what I now would describe as great cheekbones—and a gentleness that often landed him in trouble. Trouble from which his Indian sidekick, Little Beaver, would rescue him. I now know a great deal more about cowboys and beautiful cheekbones and men headed for trouble, but then all I wanted to be was Little Beaver, who I believed against all fact was a girl named Pocahontas.

Yet more, I longed to be Scheherazade. I met her first in the Classic Illustrated Comics version of the *Arabian Nights*. Many of the story panels were set in a frame of gemlike flowers and fruit. I knew each picture by heart: a genie whose glowering presence filled a whole page; the servant Morgiana, who transformed herself into a dancing girl saboteuse. Amethyst grapevines curved around one image, jade leaves and garnet berries sprung from the corners of another. The pages seemed to glimmer, as though lit from within.

Scheherazade herself was a phantasm, simply the teller of the three or four stories in the comic. I wanted more. I pursued Scheherazade to our little town library, where the library lady, more a saint than the mute statues in our church, found a children's version of the tales, a version in which Scheherazade told her own story first.

I held the book carefully to my heart, then began to read. Here was a woman who told stories to save her life, and unwittingly won the love of a powerful man. I had already learned to become the girls I read about, Mary Jemison and Jo March, Maid Marion and Joan of Arc. I knew this shape-shifting meant I was a girl who could keep herself safe for as long as there were stories to read.

Now I saw there was an even greater hope: to make up stories and to tell them—in order to save my life, and win the love of a prince.

I read the first tale, stopped and fanned open the pages of the book: three dozen stories, maybe more, a treasure chest. I would read one tale a day, for three weeks, then the book would be due. I would return it, and there would be more books, always more. In that moment, I understood the nature of perfect shelter: perfect shelter contains hope.

*The mother is gone. Someone decides the girl is old enough to visit her. They tell her she is going to a place called the state hospital to see her mother. They do not tell her the full name of the place: New York State Hospital for the Insane.*

*She is led through the big doors. Into a room that holds light that is not light. Everything is gray, the faces of the women who wear gray dresses; the whispers; other sounds that could be crying or screams, except they are eaten by the vast gray space.*

*The smell is not gray. It is not of this earth. Later her mother will come home and she will carry that odor for weeks—of terror and old, old sweat and the purple medicine the doctors give her to sleep.*

*The girl asks to be taken back to the waiting room. "Don't you want to see your mother?" someone says. The girl shakes her head. But what if her refusal kills her mother? What then?*

*"I'll see her," the girl says. At home, there are five books piled on the floor near her bed. She will go to them after this is over. They will be there. Her heart slows. She walks toward the visiting room.*

*Her mother sits on an ugly old couch. "Hello," she says. "Do you know why God hates me?"*

*The girl shakes her head. She tells herself this is only another story. Only that.*

*"God hates me," the mother says, "because I smell bad. That's why." The girl is silent. She and her mother are in a story. Only that.*

Sometime during one of my mother's winter descents, I was given a glimpse of a different shelter, one I would not find in books. It was the heart of January twilight. The kitchen window glowed soft yellow. I could smell dinner cooking. My body yearned toward warmth and food. My spirit crouched joyfully in the bitter cold.

I carved blocks from the damp snow and placed them in a small circle. I set a second row of blocks on top. I remembered the Eskimo diorama in the old museum, how a cookfire shone inside the igloo, how the huge Arctic light curved like an ice-blue bowl over the little shelter. My mother called me. I didn't answer. I sat in the imperfect shelter of my snow house. The winter sky held me in its perfect beauty.

*The girl is almost grown. On this October afternoon, she comes home to a silent house. She knows the nature of the quiet, as though the silence were an iceberg, so much of its massive cold hidden. One does not go below the surface to find the truth, one goes up, up the stairs to her parents' bedroom, where an empty pill bottle lies on the rug, and her mother is a gray sprawl on the daybed.*

*"Die," the girl whispers.*

*And she runs out of the room, down the stairs, out of the house, along the dirt path to the back of the high school where her father is finishing up his teaching day. She is running, her heart pounding against her ribs—as though words beat inside her, "So what. So what. So what."*

*And she learns that "So what" makes a shelter of its own.*

These events are a template for one childhood, for a series of true stories that were part of my training. I do not blame my parents. My mother was a witty, gifted, and loving woman tormented by the neuronal tides of her brain, her brilliance, and the stories she was told about the way to be a woman. Nothing more, nothing less, my mother's world was too often a universe of dead ends—until her seventies when death took her, then let her go. Into life. Into gratitude for the next fifteen years she lived on this earth.

My father was a frightened man, no more, no less. Control lay just beyond his reach, his wife an adorable madwoman, rich psychiatrists less knowledgeable and, in that, more cruel than witch doctors. There was no health insurance. My father worked three jobs to make ends meet. And he worried till the day he died.

My brother was a quiet boy. I still barely know him. I have searched for him for decades. In lovers. In friends. Sometimes I have found connections running deeper than blood. In all of this, I disappeared into books and was brought to life. By becoming Sacajawea and young Thomas Paine and the urchin in *Cannery Row* who teases the old "Chinaman" and meets a world beyond worlds, I became more real than myself. Becoming Scheherazade, I became the woman I am now. Light contained us—the books, the characters I occupied, the alchemized *me* reading in the blue evenings of a lakeshore winter, through long summer twilights, or by flashlight under aurora borealis spinning green silk across midnight.

# Red Canoe

■ ■ ■

In the drenched heat of a late upstate summer, my father drove our family on what seemed to be a thousand miles of northern New York dirt road into a dark pine forest. I was nine, my brother four, my young mother silent. Years later, she told me she was afraid he had taken us there to get rid of us. To this day, I haven't known if she was joking.

My father pulled the old Buick into a clearing on the shores of a tiny Adirondack lake. There was no sign of a house, no sign of anything human. I wondered if he had taken us into a fairy tale, one with bears and Windigos, the huge keening monsters of the Northern forests.

He grinned. "Follow me." We stumbled through low bushes and fallen branches to a clearing in the pines. A lake of pewter water shone at our feet. An old boat was moored at shoreline. My father stepped into it and beckoned us down.

We followed him. It was the first time I had ever been in a boat. I trailed my hand in water so clear I could see the long stems of the water lilies, and the dark lake bottom below. My father rowed us to a little island a few hundred feet from shore. A two-room shack was perched there, dwarfed by old pines and huge granite boulders.

"Here we are," my father said quietly. "Boyd's Pond."

I walked to the dock and saw a red canoe, and pale water lilies, and how light caught in the ripples moving toward me. It was like standing at the door to the library—or opening a new book. I sat on the edge of the dock. I did not need to pretend I was Mary Jemison. With the red canoe and bright water, *I* was enough.

My mother came to my side, slipped off her shoes, and sat on the dock, dangling her naked feet in the water. She lit a cigarette. I watched smoke catch on a soft breeze and drift. "Liz," she said, "this is heaven on toast points."

Now 2,200 miles and fifty-four years distant from that moment, I have an altar on the west wall of my cabin bedroom: a petroglyph rubbing from a drowned canyon, an orange *La Santisima Muerte* candle, a Mexican skeleton jack-in-the-box—and photos of my beloved dead.

My mother's picture is black-and-white. She sits on a glacial boulder at the edge of Boyd's Pond. She is perhaps forty, and she wears a white bathing suit, the straps untied, and a white fisherman's hat. Her lush breasts and elegant legs are suntanned. She smokes a cigarette. An old aluminum coffeepot sits next to her. An unbroken treeline rises on the opposite shore. I know the woman I see is happy. Unqualifiedly happy.

She is tan. She is smoking. There will be a cup of coffee. And there is sun.

If my mother was happy, I was happy. If she was happy, we were all safe. My mother was never depressed during the two weeks we swam and fished for perch, played checkers by the smoky yellow light of a kerosene lantern, watched water lilies hold dawn, glowing like the Morning Star. She, and those of us she too often despaired of loving well, seemed to be held in a thousand forms of light.

I think now of Boyd's Pond, how that dark shining water carried us. Everything made sense—whether it was pretending I could breathe in the water an inch above a granite boulder, or reading mildewed Hardy Boys mysteries I found in the little cabin. There was certainty—every morning, huge brown bass hung in the water off the dock, light fell across them, lake grass swayed beneath their still bodies. Every twilight, the lake grew absolutely still. Whippoorwills called from the shore. My father stood in the shallows, casting again and again for fish he never caught. My mother was a dark shape on a darker boulder, the tip of her cigarette a garnet.

And, always, the timeless time alone in the red canoe—floating through pale water lilies, moving so silently frogs and birds did not startle, paddling through pure dusk in a solitude that was anything but lonely—held my soul together and carried me.

For those moments, I knew I was part of something, an infinite shelter that could never be destroyed.

# The Morning in the
# Heart of the Dark

■ ■ ■

A half year later, Christmas held us in its heart. For one brief morning we were safe as we had been on that northern lake.

I have since learned how our ancestors made feasts in the icy heart of winter, putting aside enough of their precious store of food for celebration, building huge fires to encourage the sun's return, and watching through the longest night with hope and uncertainty, in hope of a new dawn.

The first thread of silver along the eastern horizon must have seemed a miracle. "Thank you," they might have whispered, afraid to frighten away the light. And then, I imagine, they went back into their caves, their hide shelters, and curled into the long winter's sleep.

My mother's heart was ancient. It moved to the implacable rhythms of the sun. She was a woman living out of modern time, not knowing her interior clock was run by light and the long, hard pull of the dark. She staved off her inevitable descent with ritual. With light and scent and baking, with ceremony that would carry her daughter for years, toward first light breaking into dark canyons, toward the moment a woman pushes through a casino's doors.

◆　◆　◆

*The girl and her brother lie warm in their beds. They have been awake for hours. Blue-black cold fills the sky outside their windows. They would dive into it naked if they thought it would bring their father's voice ringing up the stairs. Hours, days, centuries go by.*

*"Kids, you can come down now." His words are a magic spell.*

*The girl and her brother make their way down the stairs. The house is dark. They cling to the handrail and make their feet go carefully, slowly. Their full descent takes another century. They stand in the hallway. Their mother's voice comes out of the sweet dark.*

*"Wait a second."*

*They bounce on their toes. The scent of pine, of oranges and peppermint fills the hallway.*

*"Okay," their father says.*

*They step into the arch between the hall and the living room. "Merry Christmas," their father shouts. Light explodes: scarlet and green and silver shimmering in the dark branches of the tree, in the windows and on the fireplace mantel. For an instant, there are no details, only light and scent and the golden notes of "What Child Is This?" as though music was light, and their mother's fingers on the keys of the old piano, slim candles.*

*The girl lets out her breath and morning comes into focus. There are stockings and presents, and the different joy of watching her father and mother and brother open the gifts the girl has given.*

*There is a plate of butter cookies on the bookshelves, a bowl of homemade truffles on the buffet. The dining-room table is set with her mother's beloved silver, good plates, and sprigs of holly whose shining leaves and berries seem like jewels. There are mugs of hot chocolate. A bowl of real whipped cream. Sausage and eggs. WAFFLES. For once, her father says nothing when she and her brother take seconds, and thirds. He doesn't remind them how much butter costs. His generous silence seems a blessing.*

*As delicate light begins to warm the indigo morning outside the frosted windows, the girl knows the greatest joy of all. For this day, her mother is with them. She is laughing. She is calm. When she lights a cig-arette to go with her cup of coffee, her hand does not shake.*

It would be years before I understood that Christmas morning, like a contrary solstice, marked the beginning of the growing dark in my mother's brain. But then, the promise of joy seemed assured, bright as the lights on the living tree.

# Soul-Kissing in Purgatory

■ ■ ■

When does loss lead to desire? Desire to loss? When does a kiss become obsession? A touch the key that does not unlock, but imprisons? I think of a child who is rarely touched. Or told touch is a sin. I think of Catholic girls of my generation.

I was fifteen. I was luscious. I sat paralyzed with shame in the Monday Religious Instruction class of a Catholic church in Irondequoit, New York.

It was late spring of 1955 and that weekend I had allowed a boy to "go further." Which meant he had rested his hand uneasily on roughly three inches of the pleated tulle and strapless bra covering my young chest. His breath caught. "I love you," he said. I waited to feel something even better than his words—there, in my armored breasts. "I'm sorry," he said, "I shouldn't have rushed you," and took his hand away. I was silent. Not from what he might have thought, but from disappointment.

The boy was tall and lanky, with a blond brush cut and tender eyes. His first kiss had unsettled me for weeks. I wondered why girls were told that boys wanted something girls shouldn't give them till marriage. I had no idea what I wanted, but I knew that what moved in my body, what took away my appetite and made my nights wonderfully sleepless, was not the boy's, and would never be. It was fully mine. It lived in the same place as story. What bad boys wanted didn't matter.

I was not alone. My girlfriends and I invited boys to Joyce's basement rec room. We drank her mom's apricot brandy, smoked her brother's cigarettes, slow-danced to "Unchained Melody" and were baffled—and delighted—by how boys managed to walk with that long, hard thing in their pants.

The priest walked up to the blackboard and began to write. *Commandment Seven*. The boys in the class poked each other and grinned. We girls sat mesmerized, still as sacrificial maidens before the slaughter. The priest continued to write: *Thou shalt not commit adultery*. The boldest boy scribbled something on a piece of paper and passed it to the guy behind him.

"I will explain this commandment," the priest said nervously. "You all know the soul is like a blackboard. A venial sin is like a chalk mark that can be removed with prayer and penance. A mortal sin is a mark that can only be removed by time in Purgatory."

I waited. Aeons of gray Purgatory Time seemed to stretch ahead.

"Now," the young priest said, "if a woman rides horseback and gets, shall we say, pleasure from it, she commits a venial sin."

The room was silent. Everybody, sniggling boys and wordless girls alike, looked dumbfounded.

"And," our teacher went on, "if the woman gets back on the horse for more pleasure, it is a mortal sin."

Dead silence from a dozen normally rowdy teenage kids.

The priest sighed in relief and rubbed chalk dust from his hands. "I hope that clears the Seventh Commandment up for you. Next week, we will discuss the Eighth."

He dismissed us early. We did not burst from the building as we usually did. The boys walked slowly in silent groups. The girls held their books to their young bosoms and looked away from each other, and from the boys.

My friend's mom offered me a ride, but I walked home alone. I felt shattered. It was hard to breathe. The light seemed even duller than our normal lakeshore gray. I knew exactly what the priest had been talking about—impossible choices. Be good and give up the only physical warmth I'd been given in years. Be bad and give up my soul. Good. Bad. Good. Bad. I put one foot in front of the other. Good. Bad. By the time I came to Titus Avenue, I was trapped between good and bad. Between tenderness and sin.

It was just past five o'clock and traffic was heavy. I looked to my left and thought, It would be easier to die. I lifted my foot to step in front of an oncoming car. Before my foot touched down, I felt an unsought and most welcome clarity move in me like a good strong breath. I jumped back. "No," I whispered. "No."

In that instant, I left my father's church. I could hardly wait for my next date with my boyfriend. This time, I guided him. This time, when he apologized, I put my hand gently over his mouth and whispered, "Guess what comes next?" This time we moved in Animal Time, at the slow, slow pace of our wise young bodies, in what seemed an endless unfolding of pleasure.

I became a good bad girl. An A student who loved her lover's mouth on her breasts. The editor of the high school newspaper who knew that power lay in words—and in the way I could make a boy lose control.

For the first time in my young life, I deliberately chose paradox, and in that choice, saved my own life. I was shameless. A girl on her way to being a difficult woman, a girl on her difficult way. A girl who could not have guessed at the way connection can become disconnection, especially when the connected one lives in a world that fears shameless women, a world that tells them their pleasure is not theirs. A girl who, if you had told her she would spend forty years doubting her body and using men's desire to keep a false faith, would have laughed in your face.

# Kidnapped

■ ■ ■

My mother continued in her dreadful cycle. Thirty years later they finally diagnosed her as bipolar depressive. By then, she had gone through two near-death experiences and emerged lucid, cranky, and more than a little graceful. "Liz," she said, "there was nothing high about the highs. All they did was make me furious—my brain going a million miles an hour and nowhere for me to run except around the house—doing all that friggin' cleaning." She narrowed her eyes. "You know how your dad was."

How my dad was—was jealous. He did not want her to work outside the home. She was a jazz pianist with perfect pitch. She could not teach me perfect pitch, but she did teach me rhythm. Not so much from her sure hands on the piano keys, but in the ferocious largo of my response to her illness: TERROR—HOPE—RELIEF, TERROR—HOPE—RELIEF.

Musicians call the essence of a piece "the hook." It is the ineffable uh-huh that goes straight into the cells of a listener. Compelling them to move. Tarantella. The Blues. I was hooked. Unwitting. The hook so delicate and deep I didn't feel it.

During the years that my mother's depression swung through its implacable cycles, I gradually lost hope—that home would be restored, that my mother would ever again become true shelter. By the time I moved fully into my first boyfriend's arms, all that was left was TERROR, and that reduced to terror by my being very, very good—at schoolwork, at friendship, at volunteering, at making love—and at telling myself stories that alchemized a boy into a prince I could adore.

The boy-prince's desire seemed to obliterate what was left of the terror. As he kissed me and asked for touch, I believed I was safe. Then, as though his hunger were heroin, I became habituated. Soon I found nothing in his arms. My stories to myself were flat, gray. The prince had transmuted back into an ordinary mortal.

I left my first love, found another boy, wore out my desire and my stories, left him and found another. I did not consider this sinister. What feminist writer Susan Griffin has called "the roaring within" seemed only the best, troublesome part of me—the girl who shook her fine butt to rock and roll, the girl who did the choosing. The girl with power.

The summer after my senior year, the third boy-prince and I were coming home from the drive-in movies. His story was fading; still, we had drunk a few beers and made out like minks. My boyfriend drove slowly along the dark lake road. The air was wet and heavy, a thunderstorm moving in. I was shifting gears for him so his arm would be free to pull me in close. Suddenly, I couldn't feel my body. I caught my breath, sat up straight. I seemed to be floating beside myself, disappearing. I moved away from him, pressed my cheek against the damp window, felt nothing.

"What's wrong?" he said.

"Too much beer," I said.

I slowed my breath and cell by cell restored me to myself. I had no idea what I was doing but I knew the restoration was mine alone.

I remembered a night six years earlier when I had lurched awake in panic: My mother had been in the hospital, my father downstairs watching television. As I had drifted off to sleep, a thought jolted me: *some day you will die.* I came straight from sleep. I knew the thought was true, more true than anything I knew.

I went to my father for reassurance. He did his best, said something about God and Heaven and it was too soon for a twelve-year-old girl to worry about that day. And, when the time came, I could talk to a priest. In that instant, MY FATHER became a weak little man, decidedly smaller than Death. And I felt myself disappear. What was *no longer little Mary Liz* thanked her father, kissed his cheek, and climbed the stairs to her bed.


My boyfriend was quiet. I watched moonlight glint along the shoreline. There was nothing I could tell my lover. Nothing he could give me. There was only my sense that whatever had kidnapped me from myself was a mystery. And only mine.

# USING

# Smoke: Visible Vapor Given Off by
# a Smoldering Substance

■ ■ ■

To write the next ten years of my young womanhood is to write from inside a column of smoke. Chaos theory ruled. I hid in sleep. Danced mostly in fantasy. Awake, I seemed to stumble to the arrhythmia of Planxty, the ancient Irish music that constantly changes tempo.

I went ninety miles away to college, the farthest I had ever been from my parents' home, and woke in the dorm room one midnight, disappearing into terror. I seduced a young poet in order to feel safe. I was put into the dorm for "troubled" girls. I married the poet and found he was no medicine at all.

I was diagnosed: An hysteric. Suffering from panic disorder secondary to adjustment problems. Highly manipulative. Hypersexual. I was one of many young women so diagnosed. And so dismissed.

This might be closer to the truth. I was a wild kid in a young woman's body. I was a terrified girl. Scheherazade with no stories.

Perhaps you know. Because you remember your own displaced girlhood, or the days you were a young man vowing never to grow old and frozen. How you read faces and studied eyes and learned, unwittingly, to survive. And, in those lessons, forgot how to live. Except in disconnection. In a fog of marijuana, bad wine, speed racing in your blood, blurring whatever lay outside your mind—or in the "You've Really Got a Hold on Me" of what you believed was love.

I hunt through old photos and find a picture of my young self. By the time this picture was taken by my second husband, I had sleepwalked and jangled my way through the earlier marriage to the college poet and, in an act more merciful than I understood, left him and our baby. I had fled to a new man, and when he left, run straight into the second marriage, and a second child.

The photo is now on the wall above my desk. In it, I was twenty-two. I wore a corduroy smock over a plaid cotton shirt, and if you don't know the real story, you would think you saw a rounded sexy woman with smoky eyes.

In fact, the woman in the picture was two months pregnant with her third child and had such a thorough case of hay fever she could hardly see. I take the picture from its folder and hang my miserable, beautiful young self above my rolltop desk. I see a woman who lived in pure reaction. She was appetite and escape. Not smoke, but a small flame. It would be six years before she made a thought-out decision. Each morning was the beginning of her life. Each morning was the beginning of dancing around terror. Tarantella. The Blues. The hook so delicate and deep it could not be felt.

# The Windows in the
# Gypsy Wagon Are Sheets of Mica

■ ■ ■

The smoke-eyed young woman in the corduroy smock is framed by leaves, as though she stands in the heart of an Eastern woodland. In fact, she is outside a brick tenement at the corner of Fifty-second and Ellis in early-sixties Chicago. What grows around her is some tough urban weed. She and her husband are friends with drug dealers and train conductors, absurdly wealthy art collectors and artists living on tomato soup they make from ketchup. Blues bodhisattva Paul Butterfield, under the divine guidance of Ripple and reds, threatens to blow up their apartment. Her vaguely Buddhist husband gives him a joint and guides him sweetly out the door.

She cannot imagine living anywhere but in a city. She cannot imagine living more than a block from storefront gospel churches and the communion of good barbecue. She gives birth to her third child, a round, rosy girl, in the living room of their ghetto apartment. Her husband brings her Chinese food. She eats chicken fried rice, holds her daughter to her breast, and watches her husband feed their eighteen-month-old son. She knows she should feel happy.

A month later, she is in the thrall of mastitis. She fever-dreams. Her daughter cries to be fed. In Cuba, Soviet missiles are aimed at America. She doesn't care. Because in the sweet haze of fever, she imagines a lover from her past and is with him.

She and her husband go broke, go desperate, and move back to her hometown. They travel by coach on the old New York Central. She wakes before the children, whispers to her husband that she is going for coffee. The dining car is warm and quiet. A tall waiter brings her silver pitchers of coffee and real cream. Without her asking—she could not have asked, there is so little money—he brings her a fresh-baked roll, butter, and a pot of orange marmalade. She sits alone. Eats. Drinks the strong, dark coffee. Outside the dining-car window, there is old snow and gray ice piled against the shores of Lake Erie. She can't remember feeling so peaceful, so complete.

The waiter brings her bill. "No hurry," he says. "I seen you with those babies. A mama needs a little time of her own."

When she makes her way back to her family, she realizes she has no idea how long she's been gone. The children are still asleep. Her husband gazes out the window. She hands him his coffee. For that moment, she loves her life.

A few months later, she and her family are in a first-floor apartment in an old house on a Rochester ghetto street. The windows have stained-glass panels, all glowing oak trees and sail-boats and a road curving toward a radiant horizon. Cock-roaches scuttle away from the dappled light.

She gives birth to a fourth child, switchbacks through what a clinic doctor blithely calls "baby blues," lies down to sleep with terror, wakes with that most constant companion. A year later she emerges from a spiral of foggy choices to find herself and her family living in a five-room shotgun cottage a block from Lake Ontario, a two-minute walk toward a pure expanse of wild, watery light.

As summer moves in, as the easy northern evenings hang on for hours, she takes her babies to the beach. There, on an old crazy quilt, she reads everything, fine novels, potboilers, chipper housewives' magazines. Her husband brings her patchwork poetry chapbooks from San Francisco and New Orleans and the East Village. There are manic collages, quotes from Jean Cocteau, and sentences alluring as this: *The windows in the gypsy wagon are sheets of mica.*

She is not mystified by mineral windows. She has seen the world through a wavering lens, light rippled or quartz bright. She understands *she* is a gypsy wagon, her eyes windows. For a moment she is neither crazy nor absolutely alone.

Her hand, as though dancing to Planxty, writes:

*June 7, 1965: Rain on the scarecrow rosebushes outside the bedroom window, the scent of fish and wild water drifting up from the lake. The children call, forgetting I have walked into the bedroom.*

*There are a few last flickers of lightning. The sun is freed, melts hailstones glimmering in the grass. The kids stand at the front door. Matt, the baby, pisses enthusiastically.*

*Hot sun at the beach. Six lean teenaged Honda riders, roaring along the cliff above the beach. I sit on a driftwood log. Matt stuffs sand in his pockets. Sun catches in his hair. His head is a dandelion puff.*

When she sends out her poems to Beat poetry magazines, they seem to disappear. For months. A year. As though she were an ancient Japanese, writing poems to the beloved dead and setting them burning on a black river. Until, finally, an editor writes back, *You're a cool writer, but who wants to read the work of a hip housewife?*

Her husband works long hours, comes home to what he believes are the sacraments of pot and peyote, makes art, makes the astonishing beauty in his mind visible. She goes to the beach, to the storms and sun, as she would to a lover.

And then, as autumn moves in blue and brilliant, she goes to a human lover. He is another poet. He, like so many of the beautiful boys of those times, cannot stay and cannot leave. Her husband hitchhikes west, refinds a woman he once loved.

The woman's new lover flees. She does not know how to be alone. She drives her children and her self west, meets her ex-husband in Chicago, they continue on to San Francisco, where a week later, her poet calls and she loads her children and her few possessions in the car and switchbacks east.

To find herself minus the poet, in a two-bedroom ghetto apartment on welfare—at which she works harder than she has at any job other than writing. Surplus food lines, waiting hours to talk to a social worker about some administrator's mistake, stretching three weeks' worth of food and money into four. Some days the only value she finds in her life is baking bread she makes from surplus lard, flour, sugar, and oatmeal.

The poet is a brief tide in and out of her bed. He brings good mid-sixties LSD. She swallows it twice. The first time she learns there is more than one way to look at life, the second, that she is to never take acid again.

There are months of flashbacks, yearlong days of terror, of thinking she has forgotten how to breathe, and longer nights awake, fantasies of knives and blood, bleeding children howling in her mind. She sits for hours, left hand holding right, so she will do nothing terrible.

She takes herself to clinic psychiatrists. They are all men. One of them barely speaks English. They tell her she suffers from repression. Her pleasure is a sham. She is a girl-woman. A frozen child. She must find a partner, find a man with whom she can have a vaginal orgasm, become a real woman, become a wife, grow up and care about what real women care about.

Still, one morning she pulls herself out of her chair, unclenches her fist, goes to the cupboard for flour and oatmeal and lard. She brings down the old blue bowl. Her hands are clumsy, but in an hour, bread dough rises in the sun on the eastern windowsill. She cannot do more. Not just then.

She stays alive. She writes poems filled with sorrow, reads Kenneth Rexroth's translations of the thirteenth-century woman poet Chu Shu-chen, and knows it is possible for a woman to lose a great love and turn the loss to beauty.

She listens to music again. Smokey Robinson. The Ronettes. Her children play at her feet, or in the dusty alley outside the curtained windows. Somehow, ugly as she knows herself to be, men arrive and leave. She holds their empty bodies. Her hands are filled with desperation.

And then Michael Rounds appears. A wiry guy with red hair, great cheekbones, and enough gentle patience to stay with a woman who asks him, again and again, "Why are you still with me? Why?"

His answer confuses her. "I'm here because I want to watch you become as beautiful as I see you."

Michael is the most father her children will ever have. A man in love with them, with jazz, with joy, and a woman so far from joy that he shines like a distant candle in her eyes. Reflecting. Reflected. A man whose real name might be Hope.

There is at last a woman psychiatrist, a true healer, who refuses to admit the woman to a psych unit. The woman calls her the Enforcer, begs to be tucked away somewhere safe, where she won't hurt what she loves. The Enforcer says, "If you are so crazy, I guess you better put yourself into the state hospital," and when the woman says, "I can't. My mother . . . ," the Enforcer grins, a smile that seems to shift from mean to loving to amused. "You know," the Enforcer says, "you have more choices than your mother had. You have more choices than you might imagine."

The woman has no idea what the Enforcer is talking about. Because always, always, woven through the words, through the woman herself, like a filthy thread, is the conviction she is going crazy, she will end up in that gray place, in a gray dress, breathing air so gray it might as well be smoke.

There is another thread, red as a ghetto heartbeat. The thread is her writing. She can barely sense it, but when she does, it weaves a fabric stronger than fear.


*Her* writing. *The woman.* Abandoning myself to third person does not ease the sorrow that resurfaces as I remember those years and give them shape. I make myself come to *her* story again and again, though all I want to do right now is run away to Vegas, get a job as a casino buffet hostess, disappear into the sweet light of the slots; go back on e-mail, into perky cyber-code, and forget about writing in three dimensions, forget about writing the midden of a soul.

# God Is Coming and She Is Pissed

■ ■ ■

My soul gleamed. I couldn't see its light. I look back now to a rough jewel shining in a rougher setting, a smart, scared woman of the late fifties and early sixties. A bohemian. A hipster. A beatnik living in a time when the highest praise a hip cat would offer a woman was *She's a real gone chick. So cool she's ice.*

I was not alone. I met my sisters on the streets. San Francisco. Chicago. The inner city of Rochester, New York. We looked past our deliberately chill faces, locked eyes, and knew each other in a wild heartbeat.

There was Jenny, who made patchwork skirts and told stories to go with each patch. "This green near the hem, that's when Richie and I lived by a waterfall near Watkins Glen for a month; that red velvet is from my mom's cocktail dress, the stain is booze."

There was Mad Maeve, who wore a dozen necklaces every day and none by nightfall, because she believed if she gave you one, she gave you hope. There was the Black Dyke, who said, "I am a Black Dyke and I am here to tell you God is coming and she's pissed off"; who went with me to buy respectable dresses and medium-heel pumps at the Salvation Army so we could stand in front of Woolworth's on Fifty-third Street in Chicago and hand flyers to shoppers urging them to boycott the chain, so that Negroes could sit at a lunch counter in a Down South Woolworth's and eat a lousy burger.

We took the world apart. We made and unmade. We read *On the Road,* and it never occurred to some of us that we were less free than those wild Beat boys—though we caught crabs from them and got pregnant and were found dead in back alleys, or half-dead in marriages to alky painters who fucked our best friends.

We read our Scheherazades: Diane DiPrima and Lenore Kandel and Carolyn Forché. And we knew that if we were crazy, we were in lustrous company. We would not become the women our mothers were. We would not fade away.

I wonder where we are now. How many of us made it through. *Through.* Or detoured. Found an easier way around. Even if it meant a kind of disappearing.

I wonder how many of my sisters lived then, as I did, in paradox. In 1960 I rode alone across country with an imperfect stranger, lived alone on the streets of North Beach, in a single room in an ancient Chinese hotel that smelled of ginger and opium, slept wherever anyone would give me shelter, held out my hand to perfect strangers, smiled, and said, "Spare change?" A year later, I could not leave our house without my husband by my side.

I made love in a car rocketing along a wild coastal highway, and saw through the open window, as though frozen in light, a white horse on a moon-silver hillside. Months later, I could not remember how desire felt. Was it silver? Was it sea?

I fed and bathed and held my babies—and believed I was fools' mother, a woman of stone, false as pyrite. I wrote poems every day—and I believed I was not *really* writing.

And those women who were not paradoxes, who lived fueled by raw fire, shoved hand copies of their poems at you on the street, lived the pure flat busted that sent them on the streets to sell blow jobs, to the desperation that closed their throats around pills stolen from a doctor's bag, pills that might have been sweet fog or poison—their ghosts haunt me. Crazy. Inspired. Beyond survival into alchemy.

Janis. Your wildgrass hair. Cascades of beads as though you draped a waterfall around your neck. Your wail. Street cat in heat. Your dying. Not a sacrifice, but a last whisper to your sisters: Beware.

We are here, bright ghost. You know who we were, and who we are. Scheherazade's lineage, telling our stories to stay alive.

# Chief of Police Nixes
# Naked New Yorkers

■ ■ ■

By the time I turned twenty-eight, beatniks were hippies, hippies were peaceniks. America was filled with wild kids hunting a new home ground, and the possibility of greater family. My lover Michael, my kids, and I lived in an urban anarchist agrarian commune in the heart of Rochester. We described it to ourselves that way, completely without irony.

We built raised-bed gardens, organized a neighborhood food co-op, started the free school, and brought the Living Theater to town (a project that was financially doomed until the local paper's headline: CHIEF OF POLICE NIXES NAKED NEW YORKERS). We shared income. Shared housework and cooking, till the night the bearded socialist sociologist served us hot dogs baked in Ripple wine, and was relegated for eternity to washing dishes.

Michael worked for a printer, then bought a little hand-set press and moonlight-printed for our revolution. I worked as an activities director in a nursing home under Susan Reynolds, the woman who first taught me about real compassion, how holding a terrified old woman's hand meant more than filing a report on the act. When I tried to organize the staff, I was told by our boss, a grimacing man whose body seemed to contain no bones, that my services would no longer be needed.

I hit the streets looking for work. On my first interview, the director of the city health council looked at my three-entry résumé—office temp, cocktail waitress, and nursing home activities director—and said, "Why don't you tell me who you really are?"

I did. As little as I knew.

And I didn't. I couldn't tell him how my pleasure had vanished. How terror had returned abruptly one summer afternoon, the elm branches above the commune porch threatening to fragment in front of my eyes. How could I tell a stranger about the sleepless hours after midnight and before dawn in which I held each thought together, wondering when my hold on sanity would finally break? Alcohol deepened the chaos. Pot was a nightmare. I gave them up. And still there seemed no way to disconnect from what felt like a tornado in my brain. And no way to talk about it. There was, after all, the first rule of my childhood: *You never tell.*

I had discovered I could numb my brain by working every moment I was not asleep—and earn sleep by working to exhaustion. Fifty hours at the nursing home, evenings and weekends as part of a few dozen people reclaiming the gutted inner city, full-time raising my kids.

I looked at the director's tough face, his kind eyes. The room seemed airless. I took a deep breath. The whole truth began to move from my lips. "I," I said, "I . . ." He grinned. "It's okay," he said, "I think I can guess. *You* need something for your brain to do."

He sent me back to college. I went. Under Lyndon B. Johnson's Great Society program. With my rent covered. On food stamps. With child care. To become a sociologist; to figure out what made people be people, so we could educate them for change, so we could make revolution.

I believed I would gather with my professors and other students under the huge trees on the campus lawn. We would read and argue; we would untangle threads of meaning and follow them back to a common source. We would reweave what we found into a future in which no one would be poor, no one would be hungry, no one would be afraid, and no one would work at other than their gift.

A month into my first political science class I listened to my teacher tell us who welfare mothers were, and why it was so hard to organize them. I looked out the window to the big trees, saw the hard dull lines of the projects rising along the river. I couldn't stay in my body. I seemed to drift from the room.

To occupy memory so absolutely I could smell the scent of the neatly dressed black women around me, feel the music bless my bones. I knew where I was in memory. A few months earlier a hundred welfare activists had gathered in an old Baptist church in the ghetto's belly. A robed gospel choir walked slowly around the perimeter of our chairs, circling again and again, until the room had filled. Their voices were steady, singing over and over, "We've come this far by faith." One woman's soprano rose above the others, circling like a bright copper bird above us.

I remembered the mothers filing up to the microphone, how each of them paused, fanned herself in the wet August heat, then spoke: "I ask the welfare department to put back the hot lunches. My husband left me and my kids without a nickel." "I work ten hours a day cleaning houses to get by. Sometimes that hot lunch is what holds my kids till I get home."

I brought myself back into the university classroom and looked at the smart white doctor of political science telling us who I had been. Who, in so many ways, I would always be.

# The Myth of the Vaginal Orgasm

■ ■ ■

While there was much that was immutable, in my cells, in my story of myself, I was ready to find the next woman I could be. I would let my lost smoky self fade away. My brain would be my refuge. My difficult body would take a break.

I had learned, after all, that my pleasure was flawed. From the experts, from the doctors of psychiatry, from the guys in white coats who knew it all. I would enter their world. And, disconnect from what I had yet to learn was the flawless animal wisdom of my body.

I plunged into lectures and laboratories, into proofs and null hypotheses. I became fascinated by the circuitry of the brain, the neurology of pleasure and obsession. I rushed from classroom to laboratory to lecture hall with no idea I was headed for a homecoming.

I was registering for my sophomore year when a class listing caught my eye: *Soc 203: The Sociology of Women.* It seemed improbable. I wondered how we would spend an entire semester studying women. We just were. And besides, I didn't much like women. Most of my good friends were men. They were smarter. Plus, at any second, they could shape-shift into the next prince.

One of my commune sisters had begun to lecture us about the oppression of women. Her words made no sense to me. I was a free woman, the full-time mother of three of my kids, crying

towel and earth-mama for the commune, backbone of the food
co-op, had been a full-time worker and was now a student—and
a volunteer in a tiny and beleaguered nursing home. I made
love with a man to whom I was not married. I wrote radical
essays for our alternative paper, marched for peace, leafletted,
ran copy machines, typed (and proofread) speeches for the fire-
eyed guys who spoke at our rallies. How was I oppressed?

Still, a course on nothing but women was intriguing. I signed
on. The first day of class, our teacher, a young graduate student,
asked us to put the chairs in a circle. She looked at the dozen of
us, all women, and said, "You are the curriculum. We are the
story.

"Bring in *our* readings," she said, "magazines, books, adver-
tisements, cartoons, your own letters, whatever you think matters. There are no academic texts on this subject. On, as it
were, us."

I raised my hand. She laughed. "Just talk when you want to."

"What if we've written a little ourselves?"

"That would be the best," she said. "In fact, one of the
requirements for the course is to keep a journal. Get out your
notebooks. We'll start now."

The subject of women. No text. Only the sound of our pens
moving across paper.

Years later I would hear a gorgeous story about Gloria
Steinem. She was lecturing in the mid-eighties to an auditorium
filled with university students. She told them of her own college
experience, of never learning about women—in psychology, in
history, in literature, in anything but male myths and fantasies.
She spoke about building women's courses from the ground up,
from the ground of women's experiences. During Q&A, a
young woman asked, "Why didn't you just register in the
women's studies program?" The laughter in the room was from
the older women, a sound both bemused and harsh.

Our teacher taught from *Ladies' Home Journal,* Robin Morgan's *Sisterhood Is Powerful,* and Erving Goffman's *The Presentation of Self in Everyday Life;* from *Wonder Woman* and *The Graduate.* She told us to watch six hours of television and write what we were being shown about ourselves.

I read and listened and watched. In disbelief, in reluctant witness, then in rage. I wondered if I would be angry forever. Tendrils uncoiled from this new anger, an anger so deep it felt like a remembering of what I had always known, an anger that I understood was secret knowledge.

The tendrils connected me to my sister students, to women I saw in the supermarket, on the streets—and then to myself. I loved the words our teacher used. *Remember. Renew. Reconnect.* She said them as if they were something delicious in her mouth.

I understood I had been living a half-life. I wondered how it might feel to be whole, to inhabit more than the fragile sanctuary of external shelter—to occupy myself.

A young woman approached me after class one day. I'd watched her, found her plain face beautiful, realized she was the only woman in class who did not wear makeup. "We're starting a consciousness-raising group," she said. "Want to join?"

Three years later, I taught Behavioral Analysis of Women's Roles in the psychology department at that same university. It was a payback to that Soc 203 teacher and to my sisters in my CR group, though there was, in fact, no way in one lifetime I could ever pay any of those women back—for the moment I realized I always had lived as not quite good enough, and, therefore, had been bored by my own gender; for the news that seven bright, funny, accomplished women felt the same; for the evening we demolished two pans of brownies and a jug of rosé so we could talk about orgasms and I said that night I was sure I was frigid because I couldn't come from intercourse, and every other woman in the circle nodded, except for red-haired

Katy, who yelled, "Wait a minute. Stop right there," and pulled a flyer out of her purse and waved it in front of each of us: "'The Myth of the Vaginal Orgasm.' Get it?"

We got it.

# Fast-Forward

■ ■ ■

I fell in love with a man neither good nor bad, but deftly elusive. He was married, but he assured me that was a temporary inconvenience. I left Michael, one of the few acts I will regret till the day I die. It was a brutal disconnection from a deeply connected man. For decades, I would repeat my mistake, again and again.

I lived with my elusive man, his son, and my kids in a fine old shabby house in the middle of the city. It was perhaps predictable that in an effort to understand—no, to learn how to manipulate—the tricky workings of my lover's mind, I would major in counseling psychology. I became increasingly fascinated by what moves women and men theoretically, neurologically, pathologically. I read Freud and Rogers, Skinner and James. I read Jung and dismissed him as too mystical. I wanted explanations. Solutions. Healing that had been shaped around an armature of radical politics. The black box of the hypothetical spirit was too close to the color of a priest's robe. I had yet to see that the concept of the null hypothesis eliminated proof and, thereby, twisted research results, too often, into the realm of wishful thinking or a shot at tenure.

There were few women theorists. Certainly not in academic psychology—as I was reminded again and again. "There is no body of research on women," my professors said. No *body* of research. *Nobody.*

I skipped my senior year and went straight from undergrad to graduate student. I created Behavioral Analysis of Women's Roles and Women in Transition, an innovative evening class for women returning to college. In it, I taught the basics: how to approach research, discourse, and the minefield of patriarchal "scholarship." My students met in small groups in which they would tell their stories, in which there would be no arguing of hypotheses that would nullify their lives.

I decided at thirty-five to forgo a Ph.D., and graduated with an M.A. Blame hubris, blame my cellular inability to grasp graduate statistics. It is a decision I have never regretted. I was not rehired to teach Women in Transition, because my degree was "inadequate." I left the dubious shelter of the academy and worked as a feminist counselor and women's mental-health-care activist. I wrote "Alternative Healing" for the *New Women's Times*, a regional monthly newspaper, whose editor became my mentor and in an act of generosity beyond price, taught me sentence by sentence how to turn poetry into prose.

I volunteered at a nursing home, trained psych nurses in feminist counseling, taught women's courses at local colleges and saw thirty clients a week, led seven women's therapy groups. I hit the floor running at six A.M. and fell into bed every night after one A.M. The working single mothers of my generation reinvented multitasking—or maybe just carried on as most women have for aeons.

We wanted to do everything. Feel everything. It was the seventies. We, women and men alike, were discovering our *selves* and believed *we* deserved everything. Most of us were far from rich, but we were hip. No double-knit for us. No junk food. We were the frugal elite, leafing through the elegant mail-order catalogs that arrived in handfuls, then dozens, then a tidal wave of bright photos of forty-dollar T-shirts and distressed teak cigar boxes and the little brass rabbit we hadn't known we needed till

we saw it on page six, next to the raw-silk meditation pillow—
bought on credit.

We ate nouvelle cuisine, drank *Beaujolais Nouveau* as though
we were the *Nouvelle We*—of TV sitcoms, of the *New Yorker*, of PBS
and NPR, of *Gourmet* magazine and beautifully written opinion
pieces in the *Los Angeles Times;* the *We* of J. Crew and Crate and
Barrel and L.L. Bean's zillion-pocketed jackets for urbanites
who never set foot out of the city.

The *Nouvelle We*, in my Northeastern city of the late seventies,
were physicists and real-estate hustlers; nurses and coke dealers;
artists, carpenters, and earnest feminist counselors. *We* were
mostly white. *We* were somewhere between our mid-thirties and
late forties. *We* might be scuffling, but *we* earned enough for all
the *Nouveaux* and *Nouvelles*. Especially the *Beaujolais*.

I drank. My therapist drank. Her therapist drank. I remember sitting down with a client with a beer at my side. It is to that
young woman's credit that she quit on the spot. I hope she reads
this. If she does, *I am sorry. I don't expect you to forgive me.*

My lover cheated. I cheated, but we didn't call it cheating. It
was the days of *Open Marriage* and *The Joy of Sex* and the dirtiest
word was *guilt*. His kid and my three listened to our fights, our
fights about openness, about joy—night after night after night.
I suspect he was looking for mother. And me? A brother, an
equal, a story that wouldn't grow dull.

But, if you'd met me then, I would have told you I was making up for lost time. I was taking back what the crazy priest and
his story of the wicked horse had stolen from my body. I was
claiming my power, wreaking vengeance on the men whose
dominance and diagnoses had robbed my mother of her self. It
never occurred to me that there is not one whit of power in
seduction. Especially when it is lubricated by good gin.

My social drinking was a means to an end. My solo drinking
was poetry. There was Tanqueray in a Waterford goblet, chunks

of emerald lime and diamond ice. I poured three shots, filled the glass with seltzer, and gazed into its green light. I drank, not so much to disconnect from the growing failure of the story of my life, but to connect to a clarity I could not find within.

In winter I took my beautiful gin to my attic bedroom, snuggled into the water bed, watched Orion through the frosted windows. Summers I sat on the front stoop. The air was green as my drink. Wet. I held the goblet in my hands, pressed its perfect cold against my cheek. I waited to take the first perfect sip. Most probably, a Pete Townshend cut played on the stereo, most probably it was his hymn to temperance, "A Little Is Enough." I would breathe the scent of gin. Ginevra. Juniper. I would wait a little longer to drink, knowing precisely how the first swallow would trickle down my throat, as though I drank the light of the Arctic.

Now it is not the promises made and neglected in an alcohol haze, nor the procession of lovers, nor the bitter fights that my grown children seem to remember. What haunts them is how much I worked: sixty hours a week, sometimes more. Seven women's groups and thirty clients, all on a sliding-fee scale. Adjunct teaching at two colleges, a course for the free school, volunteering in a nursing home, at feminist conferences. I baked Xmas cookies from scratch, painted elaborate Easter eggs, cooked paella and *cacciatore* for my professor lover and his distinguished visitors. I took no vacations, no weekends.

This busyness was not about money—despite the chic catalogs piled on the kitchen table. It was only marginally about good-heartedness or politics. I was a woman disconnecting from my moments alone, when the world seemed to shatter into terror, into madness coming toward me at the speed of loss. The moments for which—I could not yet have guessed—my spirit and writing longed.

My elusive man found true love elsewhere. I learned an old

old wisdom: a guy who leaves his wife for you will leave you for the next perfect woman. His son, a lovable teenager, stayed with my kids and martyr me in the fine old house. Every morning of early spring 1978, I heard my ex's car pull up to take his kid to school, felt my heart ache, and wondered what was wrong with me. I pulled on jeans and a sweatshirt, got the coffee started, and waded into a day of convincing other women they had the right and responsibility to believe in themselves.

And then my once-lover and dear friend Michael died. Suddenly. Running along a trail in the Maine woods. His lover called: "The doc said his heart exploded between the time he brought his foot up for the next step and he hit the ground. There was no pain." Nor for me. By then there had been other deaths, other atrocities, all of them icing my heart, all of them other people's stories. That seemed reason enough to be numb. When in pain, disconnect.

I came back from Michael's funeral and settled in seriously with work, Tanqueray, and too much heartless sex with too many bodies. I wanted to check out and wake up when it—I wasn't sure what *it* was—was over. But, a woman afraid of death does not kill herself. I had long ago vowed my children would *never* go through what I had. They might come home to a lush, but never a half-dead mom.

And besides, there were my women friends, not miracles, but daily facts of sisterhood. Barbara. Joann. Fran. Char. A painter. A potter. Two healers. We did what women have always done: talked, listened, said "bullshit" when necessary. We arrived at the front door unannounced with a pound of Brie, a loaf of Italian bread, a stick of sweet butter, and a bottle of fine local wine. We left lousy relationships, dove into new ones. We painted. Sculpted. Made jewelry. Cut ski trails in new powder. One of us even, sometimes, when all else had failed, wrote.

How could she not when she had—has—a friend like Barbara. It was mid-February in the late seventies. I was still half there with the elusive man. Barbara and I sat at an antique table under hanging plants in a little restaurant on Rochester's main chictique street. I am sure we were eating Caeser salad with grilled chicken breast, which was considered cutting-edge cuisine at the time, and we were both drinking a little too much Bully Hill Seyval Blanc, a beautiful local wine made by a goaty guy who printed his own, faintly erotic labels. I was reporting, for the twentieth time, that the elusive man's other lover had called the house at three A.M. when Barbara reached across the table, took my hand in hers, and said, "I'm bored. I want to talk about something other than men."

I swallowed hard. My friend looked scared. The most basic rule of seventies sisterhood had suddenly changed. What smart, funny, terrific women did was take care of each other in their disconnections with elusive men. But the worst sin of the *Nouveau Temps* was to be boring. "Okay," I said. "What do you want to talk about?"

"Art," she said. "And writing. And I'm also bored with us doing nothing but eating lunch and talking. I've got an idea."

Two weeks later, Barbara had found a cheap loft and set up her easel. We trudged through the city's gray slush to an old warehouse, took an industrial elevator up six stories, and walked into a big icy room. Through its cobwebbed windows we could see the pewter river running north to the frozen lake. Barbara pointed me to a battered table. I took off my coat, pulled my journal from my purse, and wrote. *Pewter. Frozen. Here. What the fuck am I doing here?*

We went to work.

# Brother Blood/Sister Solitude

■ ■ ■

Nicholas walked up my sidewalk one of those long, soft, North-eastern summer twilights. He sat beside me on the front stoop, a lanky man whose huge brain and even bigger heart were as desperate as mine. And certainly as shielded.

I sipped a triple Tanq and soda; he'd brought his own generic beer. We watched white moths disappear into the glow from the old streetlights, saw them reappear against the growing dark. One moth fell toward our candle, dropped into the wax and burned. For hours. Nicholas and I said little, but by the time we moved into the house to listen to Bob Dylan's *Street Legal* and wait for me to take his hand in mine, I knew I'd met my match.

I have never been so deeply in love. Years later I would hear Aaron Neville sing "Brother Blood," and I would realize how feeble the words "in love" are. What murmured in my cells seemed to resonate in his. We were kin by connections strong as bloodlines. I missed the fact that Nick was fourteen years younger. And a century older.

He was my home ground. My body knew this. No words were necessary.

I understand now that Nicholas was not really the gift. I know it was a grace both within and without me that allowed me to open my heart to a man I knew would not stay, grace that eased me into full connection with another human being. I remember lying next to him, watching him sleep, seeing his breath move in his chest, seeing a profile as dear to me then as the clean line of desert mountains is to me now, and thinking, I will feel every particle of this moment—and of whatever comes next.

What *had* to come next was the gift of his absence. We were in our second summer together. I was forty. I had spent time alone only for as long as it took me to drive from my home to class, from women's meeting to nursing home, from my house full of kids to lunch with a pal. That did not seem unusual to me or my women friends. Most of us, gay or straight, had gone from our parents' homes to relationships; many of us from marriage to marriage to affair after affair. I'd been a mother since I was twenty, a worker far longer. And in the few moments I braved alone, terror arrived on cue.

I know now that many women of the late twentieth century lived in the same lonely, necessary chaos. Aching for our own company, afraid to find it. Raising kids alone, reading *Ms.*, reading *Essence,* rallying for women's rights, talking of sisterhood— and disconnected from the sister we would carry till the day we died. Our self.

Nicholas and I had begun to stumble against our differences. I knew we could not last. I knew I needed to prepare for a tender and absolute good-bye, so I took my anger and sorrow to a woman not so much a therapist as a healer. Nicholas did what he could.

"You need to spend some time alone," my healer said.

"Why?"

"To meet yourself." I looked into her eyes. She was the only person I trusted. I started to tell her there was nothing inside me. She took my shoulders gently in her hands and shook me. As a mother cat might shake a kitten. "Please," she said. "Stop being so quick for five minutes. Please." I slumped into her generous hug and tried to slow down. A sorrow rose in me, ran deeper than thought, wilder than my tears.

And so, in July 1980, I found myself packing my old station wagon with clothes and books and embroidery thread and a boom box and tapes and food and gin for a week in the cabin on the island at Boyd's Pond. I had enough supplies for a year. Nicholas would ride up with me and spend the night. My son and his best friend would come up later. I would spend three days alone. I was going for a personal best.

The time on the island with Nicholas was predictably hot, unpredictably sweet, and over too soon. I drove him to the main highway so he could hitch home, dropped him off, pulled a U-ey, and watched his big, beloved self shrink in my rearview mirror. His old backpack was slung on his shoulder and he'd tied a red bandanna around his black hair. "Goodbye, gypsy bro'," I whispered. I knew it was a rehearsal.

Then I came to the turn to the thousand-mile dirt road, swung the wheel to the right, and was alone, heading up into ragged Adirondack pines, toward a black lake and three days of a freedom that seemed more like death.

I kept busy with unpacking and cooking as long as I could. The long summer evening moved slowly in. I sat on a granite boulder that sloped down into the bright water, made a little fire and a big drink. I remembered how my mother would sit on the dock at dusk while my father fished the shallows. The tip of her cigarette would glow in the fading light. The wind would die, the lake go flat and bright as a silver mirror.

I heard voices from the southern shore, and laughter. I thought of Nicholas. Of work. Of making another drink. Instead, I made my bed on the front porch. So I could see the sky—aurora borealis and meteors and how, if I remembered right, dawn came up delicate apple green.

It was the first night in thirty-two years (after all, I had been my mother's mother since I was eight) I had spent without someone for whom I was responsible within range. I could not sleep. My breath caught in my throat. I felt dizzy. Coffee and gin and emptiness pounded in my blood.

To my relief, a marvelously distracting thunderstorm slammed in. Wind blasted the pines. The cabin shook. Stunned by ice-blue lightning, I held my hands in front of my face and whispered, "I'm here. I'm here." And I knew that what took my breath was not the possibility of death by lightning or any threat from outside my maelstrom brain. I counted my breaths over and over until I fell asleep.

The second night there was no storm. No bears. No distraction. I lay in my own company and when my breath caught, I followed it. For hours. Into the old familiar terror. Into no answers. No revelation of abuse. No obvious devastation. No easy release. Only, at last, a bittersweet joy that I was finally free to go *in*. To begin to connect with the dubious shelter of my own life.

When Nicholas left that fall, I fought for my life with more tenacity than I ever have and prayed I would ever have to again. I did not know how I would live without him. I told myself stories, made shelter of the possibility of his return. My fantasies were not sexual. They ended with his words "I miss you. Can we try again?"

It took eight years to stop thinking of him on a daily basis, and twenty-two to see a photo of him as a middle-aged man and realize that the man I loved so deeply was gone. Hitchhiking away on a long-ago Northern highway, his pack on his back, his wild black hair tied up in a red bandanna. And to finally wish him fare thee well.

# Burning

■ ■ ■

To live without Nicholas immediately after the separation required a thousand disconnections—from the phone, from the first step on the way to his house, from the sight of his old green truck. I stayed alive in a numbness from which I emerged, barely, to witness the city I loved almost as dearly as his presence begin to die. At first I didn't see the necrosis. It was delightful to find a new coffee shop, a pleasure to walk Monroe Avenue buying handmade candles and rosemary soap, eating in restaurants that served falafel or Pad Thai or hazelnut gelato. A local supermarket began to fill its shelves with croissants and imported Gorgonzola. I could rest from shopping in its little espresso café.

Then the pungent old German sausage shop was suddenly gone, and the Ukrainian store in which you could buy brilliant Easter egg dye, beeswax, and tools to make eggs more intricate and jewel-like than Fabergé's. The Jewish bakery closed its doors and the Sicilian place with the best greens 'n' beans in America was gone.

Gone. And worse than gone. The mom-and-pop businesses, the richly diverse neighborhoods, the scary streets and burned-out reminders of what the sixties race riots had told us we had damn well better remember were replaced by twenty-four-carat boutiques and houses painted in San Francisco mauves and lilacs. All owned by people whose skins and hearts were relentlessly lily white. I came awake to a city being gutted by money, greed, and numbing charm.

My journals from that time are gone. I burned them on the shores of a little New York lake one August night a year after my first road trip west. I had reread the journals under high-desert light and seen they were records of what alchemists called the Black Work, the time when a substance is sealed into an airless bottle and left until it has transmuted into the numinous, into the possibility of freedom.

I tore the pages from their bright bindings and fed them to the fire. Smoke rose.

When all that was left were ashes, I gathered the fine gray powder into a bright scarf, tied the bundle tight, took it home, and scattered the ashes across the black dirt of my garden. Tomatoes would thrive there. And a row of cilantro I planted as a promise to my Southwestern future.

I was learning to let go. To disconnect.

From Nicholas. From a home that had ceased to be home.

These disconnections were different. They were conscious, gifts that taught me to love the *rituals* of letting go. The launch. The flight. The looking back and seeing one is free.

I will probably never learn to love what follows. The aftermath. We need allies for the persistence, the gray gray grayness that follows the sacred fire, or tossing the lover's gift of a silver bracelet in a High Sierran river, or being the woman lying on warm sand, whispering, "Take it all." There must be companions to accompany the surrendered one into not-knowing. As she goes slowly, howling, or in icy silence.

Back then, I went into the gray in the company of women friends. In the company of sorrow and Tanqueray and hope so delicate it could have been a white moth becoming flame.

# HUNTING SHELTER, FINDING SANCTUARY

■ ■ ■ ■ ■ ■ ■ ■ ■ ■ ■ ■ ■ ■ ■ ■ ■ ■ ■

# Hunting Shelter, Finding Sanctuary

■ ■ ■

I was a single, not-quite-middle-aged woman on the prowl. Hunting shelter. Believing it would lie in the arms of a tall young guy with black hair and a crazy laugh, a guy exactly like Nicholas, a man who was the lover I was never to find again. My hunting trail was well worn. It led from one singles' bar to another. I had no ammunition, no weapon. My hunger was my bait.

I carried little more than longing into the bar of a local French restaurant in late September 1980. There was Nicholas's absence, my trust in no god I had ever met, and my persistent faith that the right man could gather the splinters of my heart and mend them. A bearded guy who looked like a stocky Pete Townshend sat at the bar. I was in love with the Who, had gulped a double Tanq and soda to ease into the evening, so I smiled at him and said, "You look like Pete Townshend."

He grinned blearily and said in a Cockney accent, "You look like Joan Collins." He meant Judy, but by the time I knew that, I'd fallen in love with the way he talked. An accent can carry infatuation only so far. We became not lovers, but friends. His presence changed my life far more than any lover ever had, or will. Not because he was shelter, but because he became my guide to the shelter that contains me to this day.

Ashley was a Cockney wild guy who loved the West so much

that when he was a kid in London, his mother gulled him into eating liver by telling him it was buffalo. Two years after we met, he popped the question that changed my life. One ice-bound two A.M., as we sat nursing my gin and his eighth beer, he said, "This summer let's go out west. You'll love it."

"Thanks, but no thanks," I said. "I've been there. Too boring, too beige, and too big."

"Just the Grand Canyon," he said.

"The Grand Canyon is Disneyland with rocks."

"I bet you fifty bucks you're dead wrong." He clinked his glass on mine.

Six months later we took off. On an Indiana six-lane, I looked around at miles of malls. "I hate the West. I want to go to Maine."

"Fifty bucks riding on this," my pal said, "and Indianapolis isn't the West."

In Colorado, Saint Mary's Glacier melted slower than time into a crack in my heart I hadn't known existed. A mountain dream later, my friend walked me, eyes closed, to the edge of Grandview Point at the Grand Canyon.

"Open your eyes," he said gently.

I did. In a heart-jolt of vast aurora rock, I was taken. Amazed. Knowing I knew nothing, and nothing was exactly enough.

I cried every day of the drive back east. It seemed unbearable to return to a world not only without Nicholas, but without huge light and mountains rising from hard desert. What had once been my beloved home seemed crowded, airless, the gray skies a catalyst for depression that would surely kill me.

"We'll come back," I said. "Next year."

"I promise," Ashley said. "Count on it."

*We* didn't go back a year later. I did—not to stay, but to reenter the solitude I had first known at the little mountain lake. I was in a new, almost welcome terror, the terror of knowing that if you don't go forward, you will sink back. On a muggy one A.M. in June 1982, Ashley and my youngest son nudged me firmly up the steps of the westbound *Lakeshore Limited*. I was certain that I was being exiled into much more of my own company than I had ever wanted.

I wedged my two bags into the rack and slid into a window seat. I was sobbing. I watched my pal and my son step under a station light. They were laughing, waving, behaving as though they might actually see me again alive. Then the train lurched, the car lights dimmed, and I felt myself moving west.

I'd chosen Flagstaff, Arizona, for my base camp because it was on the train line, in the heart of a dozen Indian ruins—a little dot in the middle of big nothing. As I sat in the dark train watching the lights of home fade behind me, it seemed as though I were launching into outer space. I tilted my seat back and closed my eyes. Remember, I thought, why you are doing this.

Two nights later, I knew. I stepped off the train into a wash of pine air and looked up at a crescent moon, at stars bright as the ones we had watched from the island at Boyd's Pond. A beat-up cab waited in the parking lot. The train hooted once and was gone. I climbed into the cab and said the name of an old down-town motel I had booked months earlier. The driver said, "No problem," and we drove two blocks. The fare was a buck. I tipped him the same and walked through the front door of the Monte Vista, into a lobby that looked as though Red Ryder would be just upstairs.

I woke next morning not in a cowboy's company, but my own. All that was missing was coffee. I headed out. Dark moun-tains, one with the perfect southern slope of Fuji, watched over the town. I smelled roasting coffee beans, followed my nose across the railroad tracks to a tiny storefront. Macy's Café. When I stepped up to the counter and saw the pastry case crammed with fresh Danishes, looked around and saw people who might have been North Beach desperadoes twenty-five years earlier, I suspected I was being made an offer I wouldn't refuse.

"Okay," I said, "I'm ready."

I drank my cappuccino. The coffee was a fierce, complicated blend I'd never tasted before. I ordered a tuna sandwich on homemade bread and a second coffee for the road. I picked up my rental car. It was dark blue. The guy at the rental desk grinned. "Blue is lucky," he said. *"Buena suerte."* He was getting off his shift. He asked me to drop him at his house. He climbed out of the car and came around to my window. "When you come back," he said, "eat dinner at El Charro. My aunt and uncle own it. It's real Mexican food. Real."

A week later I sat at the window table in El Charro. The waitress studied me and said, "Let me choose for you." She brought a bowl of steaming posole and a covered plate of fresh corn tortillas. I picked up my spoon. "Wait," she said, "not yet," and sprinkled chopped herbs over the posole. "Cilantro," she said. "Now you can eat."

I spooned the stew into my mouth. Hominy. Tender pork. Chile. And cilantro, as much color as taste, green and lemony, like nothing I had tasted before. I dipped a tortilla into the broth. Outside, night moved in, the street dark except for the taillights of pickup trucks rattling by. A Native American couple walked past the window. The light from the window shone on the woman's hair. I bit into the tortilla. Cilantro. A woman's hair gleaming like a raven wing. I knew I had crossed a divide.

Earlier in the week at the Grand Canyon, I had walked miles along the earth's hard and glowing heart. I watched specks of black spiraling up toward the rim, becoming ravens, soaring above me, becoming specks again, then disappearing. I'd been stopped on the road into Chaco Canyon by a tiny white dog barking at the front of my car. He herded three dozen goats in front of me, and when the last goat was nearly across and I began to edge forward, he jumped in front of my car and barked again.

I'd slept in the back of my car in the campground of Navajo National Monument instead of driving back to my hotel room at Hopi, because a gay nurse fed me supper and told me the ranger would take us down to Kawestima ruin at dawn. He said we have in our short lives only two choices: to be safe or astonished.

The next morning I came around the curve in the trail and looked up. The ruin, red as carnelian, was set in a three-hundred-foot-high cave in a five-hundred-foot sandstone cliff. I moved beyond astonishment, into wonder, and more. I knew just how small my life is. And how primitive my European ancestors had been.

Then, perched on a mesa above Spiderwoman Rock at Canyon de Chelly, I drank bootleg beer, ate bad Navajo tacos with a turquoise-draped New Westerner from San Francisco, and heard her say in an unadulterated Brooklyn accent, "Honey, the way you seem to love the West, you ought to read *The Monkey Wrench Gang*. It'll change your life."

I headed back to Flagstaff a day early. I wasn't sure why. I was driving between two ranges of the Jemez Mountains in brilliant sunlight. Lightning storms jittered over the indigo peaks on either side of me. I was listening to Pete Townshend's "Empty Glass," astonished at the complete absence of fear in my heart, when I understood I was free. To leave my worn-out home. Alone. To spend, if it played out that way, the rest of my life mostly in my own company. With no guarantees.

And the price of that freedom was going to be just about everything.

I spent the extra day in Flagstaff walking the little town. On old Route 66, I found Winter Sun, a trading post filled with herbs, silver, and spirit, run by a slender black-haired woman with a wild laugh. We talked about women's health. About living free. I told her I felt as though I had come back from the dead.

"Go to the mountains," she said. "They're sacred to the local tribes. White people call them the San Francisco Peaks." I started to tell her I didn't believe in woo-woo stuff. Then she grinned and laughed her street-witch laugh, and I trusted her.

I walked north up the long hill toward the mountains and watched in perfect cynicism and trust as clouds moved across their dark flanks. "Whatever you want," I whispered. I had no idea I was praying.

I remembered the wiseass oracle at Canyon de Chelly, and seeing a bookstore near Macy's. I found the jam-packed rooms of Aradia Bookstore, bought my first copy of Ed Abbey's *The Monkey Wrench Gang*. "There are chairs in the front room," the owner said. "Take a break." I settled into a fat purple bean bag. A big malamute wandered in and stretched himself out next to me. I opened my book. An hour later I knew the woman on the edge of Canyon de Chelly had been right.

I stopped at the local newspaper office and bought a six-month subscription. That night I read the want ads, saw rents I could afford and jobs that used hands instead of head.

I read a few more chapters of Abbey's book and drifted into sleep more peaceful than I had known since the nights next to Nicholas's body—nights that seemed as though they had occurred in another lifetime, another world.

Next morning I picked up Macy's coffee and a cardamom-pear Danish on the way to the train. I sat in the lounge car, drinking the fine, dark brew, smearing butter on pastry still warm from the oven. I watched the sacred mountains grow smaller and smaller, till the train and I were beyond their range—and I knew they waited, patient as stone, in my heart.

# How to Leave: Leave

■ ■ ■

Back home in the Northeast, I felt like a ghost. By our gray light, I read any book on the Southwest I could find, let the memories of silver dawns and mineral sunsets flood my spirit. It took eleven months of letting go of almost everything except the old house and my grown kids before I looked around my near-barren attic sanctuary and knew I was really saying good-bye. There had been the yard sale, the odd joy of watching people walk away with things I had once absolutely had to have. There was the ritual of checking the phone machine, sure Nicholas would have heard I was leaving and called to beg me to stay.

There was the endless round of sad lunches. My women friends somehow managed not to disconnect before we disconnected. I was less faithful, in many ways gone before I left.

And unexpected, there was a perfect moment, so like the perfect lovemaking that can sometimes occur with a lover we know we must leave. I sat at the edge of my garden at sunset and saw the last of the tomatoes glowing like scarlet lanterns. I picked one, bit and swallowed. All the lush juice of a rain-belt summer flooded my mouth. Time stopped. Memories sheltered me. I bit again into the tomato, the salt of my tears perfect with its sweetness.

Three weeks before launch, I forgot the words of the gay nurse and the oracle at Canyon de Chelly and the dark-haired herbalist in Arizona. I was amnesiac for lightning over the Jemez Mountains and the long cobalt sweep of the sacred peaks. I even forgot the best coffee I had ever drunk.

I forgot everything except the hard price of my easy twentieth-century American white girl freedom. I was paying dues, so scared my breath caught in my chest and my eyeballs shook. I couldn't read, couldn't sink into the perfect death-in-life of three movies in a row on the VCR.

My mind raced. Nothing, not gin, not last-ditch efforts to reach Nicholas, nothing worked. A few weeks before my voluntary exile, my son Sam found me sitting at the kitchen window staring out at the cold Northern light. I was thinking that maybe no sun for months, and Nicholas gone forever five blocks away, was just what I needed. It sure beat living the rest of my life in psychosis.

"What's wrong?" he asked.

"I'm wondering who I'll turn to for support out there."

"Jeez, Mom," he laughed. "It's not Mars. Besides, what are you going to need support for? You've got enough money to live on for six months without working. You've got everything you need."

I looked up at him. I couldn't speak what formed in my mind: *I'm going into nowhere with nothing but what I've left undone.*

But I knew he was right. A college boy had rented me a little stone house in the heart of Flagstaff for no more than my word that I was on my way. I had enough to live on for six months. I was going into a world in which I knew no one, and no one knew me; a world in which the battle to say no to yet another request for my time would be over. And I still had terrific legs.


December 27, 1984, I finished leading my women's group, dropped my datebook in the trash, and settled down for the last night in my waterbed. I couldn't sleep. I wanted to haul the datebook out of the trash, write something, anything, in the squares for the next few weeks, as though responsibilities would be a kind of map. I didn't. I imagined walking through the blank white squares, as though through desert. I fell asleep hours later with nothing but emptiness stretching ahead.

The next morning Ashley and my grinning son helped me cram the last possible box into the U-Haul. Sam eyed my gypsy wagon—my beloved 1980 Firebird and U-Haul medium trailer. "If you don't got it, you don't need it," he said.

I almost said, "I need you. And your sister. And your brother. And the possibility of Nicholas. And the guarantees of Barbara and Char and Joann and Fran. And the certainty of great barbecue, blues, and long, long summer twilights. "I didn't. Not because it wasn't true, but because it was.

I climbed into the driver's seat. Ash rode shotgun. I backed out of the driveway into the slushy street. I'd planned it that way. It was time to do what I wasn't good at: maneuver backward hauling a trailer, look up openhearted at my kids standing on what was no longer my porch, see them wave and laugh and raise their right fists in the air, say good-bye, feel my heart break and know it was because it held a lifetime of love—and regret.

I sobbed as though I were the one being left. I looked down the little street, drove slowly toward the intersection that led north to Nicholas's shack, south to what came next. I turned south.

Twenty minutes later, still sobbing, I drove down the ramp to the New York State Thruway and swung the Firebird onto the road. I felt car and trailer leap forward. I raised both fists in the air. Ash grabbed the wheel.

"Good-bye," I shouted. My tears stopped instantly and absolutely. I took hold of the wheel.

"I did it, Ash," I said. "It's done." I heard myself, and realized I spoke not so much to my friend, as to myself.

# I'm Scared. I'll Do It.

■ ■ ■

Eight days later I drove into Flagstaff to Bonito Street. It was a brilliant mountain morning, I parked in front of the little stone house that was to be my home. Chunks of black glass glittered in its outside walls. There was a fireplace chimney and a tiny porch. A train hooted just far enough from the bedroom window. And a few miles north of my front stoop, the sacred mountains rose against an ice-blue sky.

I stood in the bright living room and felt a grin on my face. I've come to know that smile well as I've sifted through quartz pebbles on the shoreline of Fossil Creek; paddled into an easy rock-and-roll rapid on the San Juan, my body part of the boat, the boat part of the river; as I've run down a limestone slope a half mile from my home to see snowmelt racing through an old meadow's gully. That morning, standing in an empty house that would soon be filled with what bits and pieces of myself I had carried across 2,200 miles and eight days, I touched my smile and whispered, "Thank you."

I had a few ideas of how I might begin to spend my time. There was, of course, finally, at last, at long last, writing, really writing, really writing real writing. There were ancient ruins everywhere, mapped and unmapped; dozens of equally intriguing small-town streets; coffee and cardamom Danish—and there would be, sure as a forty-five-year-old woman's desire, men. Real men. Monkey wrenchers. Brilliant Vietnam vets who loved the sun-cooked rock and manic white water, hated progress and knew how to stall a dozer in its tracks.

Ed Abbey had told me there would be guys like that. *The Monkey Wrench Gang* and *Desert Solitaire* had become topo maps for my heart. I had followed them to this moment, this grin, these next words, "Let's get breakfast, Ash. Then I'll unpack."

I drove Ash to the Phoenix airport three days later, dropped him off and headed north. I was as alone as I had ever been in my life, except perhaps in the long hours of birthing my children. Even the Terror was gone. That seemed astonishing. But no more so than the moment I curved down the long hill into the Verde Valley, saw the peaks rising against the twilight, and realized I was thinking, I'm home.

The air was luminous, sheer layers of its bluepinkviolet. The mountaintops were rosegold in last light, as though carved from fire agate. I decided to take a detour into the desert around me—because I was afraid to—and pulled off on a rutted dirt road. I took off my seat belt, rolled down the window, and drove past clumps of scented trees and little washes that glowed scarlet in the ember light. I wondered what I would do if I got stuck, cursed myself for not bringing gallons of water, cookies, and a signal flare. I kept driving, kept looking, kept breathing in scent I had never smelled before, the delicate musk of desert twilight.

A dark shape appeared at the side of the road. I slammed on my brakes. What appeared to be a chunky pig in high heels minced across the road. My heart bumped against my ribs. Later I would learn the pig was a javelina. And the breath catching in my throat not fear, but wonder. *I'm scared. I'll do it.* became my passwords.

I managed to live outside datebook time for a few weeks. I ate when I was hungry, walked when I felt restless, stayed still when it was the last thing I wanted to do. I slept till my body woke, took naps, fell asleep when I needed to. I realized I was exhausted.

I bought a little black-and-white TV and tried to watch it one night. I knew it was my last grasp at certainty, at filling hours better left as empty—at disconnection. I looked at bloodless ghosts jitter on the screen and felt as though I kept company with a vampire. I took the TV to Goodwill the next day.

My sense of pure grace lasted a month. Then, despite more sun than I'd seen in any Eastern summer, despite pine forests through which I skied new tracks in brilliant snow, despite the best mom-and-pop Mexican food I'd ever eaten, I found my days too long and far too lonely. I would have run back home, but every time I thought of giving up, I felt like I was dying.

I wrote letters, checked the mail every five minutes, cursed the unblinking eye of the phone machine. I even considered replacing the television.

A mountain blizzard brought me to my senses. We were snowed in for what seemed forever. I woke the second day before dawn with hours of nothing but my own jittery company ahead. I made coffee and waited for the reliable jolt. It didn't work. In desperation, I switched on the radio to NPR's *Morning Edition*. I heard the eerie space-music of *Star Date*. I learned about ice and dust, light-years farther away than Rochester, New York, and somehow felt closer to home. I listened to the local announcer tell us schools were closed. "Have fun, kids," he said. I pretended he was talking to me and took down my skis.

Next morning I turned on the radio before I got out of bed. And the next morning. And the next. Feeling safe long enough to begin to venture out up the northern highway to camp in Arches National Monument and hike a three-mile trail with no water, a dehydrated greenhorn, wondering why I felt stoned, why I kept stubbing my toe. I walked into Flagstaff's downtown and found Choi's, a diner that served huge sweet rolls with terrifying Day-Glo pink jelly in their hearts. On the South Side, I refound Aradia, the little bookstore I had discovered on my solo trip. Its shelves were packed with women's stories; one of the finest collections of work by and on Native Americans in Arizona; and, in the big front room, everything Edward Abbey had ever written.

There were those soft bean-bag chairs, and welcome-home light pouring in through the huge windows. The malamute greeted me. I settled in till the owner, a big woman with a pure Irish grin, began to close up. I rapidly reduced my nest egg by a hundred bucks, came home with a half dozen books by Abbey and Terry Tempest Williams, and moved joyfully into my long winter nights alone.

And not so alone. Halley's Comet drifted above Ed and Terry and me. I hiked up Mars Hill and watched the old, old light-seed through the Lowell Observatory telescope. I watched Orion and his prey, the star-rabbit Lepus, proceed across midnight, read a book on Native American astronomy and learned the Hopi believed the star warrior was the head of a giant hero. *Hotomquam.*

# Heading Home

■ ■ ■

I began to volunteer at Wupatki National Monument, the ruins of an old Hopi city north of Flagstaff. I worked at the front desk a few weeks till the fifth tourist asked me if the ruins were worth the 1,500-foot walk on a paved path to reach them, and I knew I had not come west to sell people on the possibility of amazement.

Steve Cinnamon, the resource manager, adopted me. We poked through the ruins, pulled up nonnative oats, replanted pine trees. He told me how it might have been to have lived here, to have called this hard beauty home ground.

One afternoon we found tourist garbage at a little ruin, picked up crumpled beer cans, scrubbed away graffiti vows of love and vengeance. Steve cussed. I walked out into the black sand, picked up a pottery shard, and held it in my palm. Red clay, white glaze, a web of delicate black lines. Steve held out his hand. "The artist painted that with a yucca brush and an extract of bee weed," Steve said. "Maybe she was the last person to touch it. Eleven hundred years ago."

I turned the shard in my palm. It seemed proof of magic so simple, a woman could shape it from earth. It seemed a message from the past, a message for the future. Steve had told me the early Hopi sent runners to carry the news. I took off my hiking boots and dug my bare toes into the sand. I closed my eyes. For an instant, I pretended I was running. Carrying the shard.

Steve's shadow fell across the red light behind my closed lids. "You have to put it back," he laughed. I set it down in its hollow in the sand and I wondered if it would ever again be touched by other than wind, rain, or lizard.

"Let's go back," Steve said, "into the future." We climbed into his work truck and rattled back to his research office.

Steve put me to work entering data in a computer. It was the first time I had ever touched one. Its light seemed icy, its efficiency seductive. He told me it contained chips of information. I remembered the shard. I understood that what appeared on the screen were messages made from light. And I was the runner. Heading, though I couldn't have guessed it at the time, toward home.

I was reading a research paper on the early residents of Wupatki when a sentence leaped out: *The people of the tribe welcomed children; there was high infant mortality, and many hands were needed for hunting, gathering, and farming.* I copied the words in my notebook.

That night, at what was not quite yet home, I wrapped up in my sleeping bag and sat in the backyard under Orion's broad and shining shoulders. I watched him stalk across the sky. I understood that he headed toward the Hopi mesas and that when he reached them, there might be those who would look up and see Hotomquam. I remembered the sentence about women in the research paper and found myself thinking, What would happen to an ancient Hopi woman who could not have children?

There was no answer from the star-giant above me. There was only the question. And the memory of a vow I had made in a time that seemed light-years away.

It had been the bone-damp winter a year before I moved west. Nicholas's absence was more fierce than the minus-10-degree wind chill outside my attic bedroom. I'd reread *The Monkey Wrench Gang* for the third time, *Desert Solitaire* for the fifth. The books had kept me alive. They carried me into the possibility of light, into the probability of scarlet rock and easy silence. They taught me I could not live in that besieged beauty casually.

I sat on my bed by candlelight, Orion's dagger just visible from the eastern window. I polished off a bottle of fine Bully Hill Seyval Blanc, burned the last of the juniper I had brought from Arizona, and talked to Ed Abbey.

"Ed," I said, "I'm coming west. I'm going to write and fight for the earth. I promise."

And then I put on my headphones, cranked up the fool's anthem of "Tracks of My Tears," and cried myself to sleep.

The memory faded, gone much farther than two years and 2,200 miles, becoming less than stardust. Only my vow still burned. *I will write and fight for the earth.*

The westbound train howled into the Flagstaff station a few blocks from where I sat. I thought of my vacation two years earlier and how solitude and the westbound train had brought me to this beginning, and to the question: *What would happen to a woman of the tribe who could not have children?* I wrapped the sleeping bag tighter around me. I was as lonely for Nicholas as I had been. But the cold that held me did not cut to the bone. The question warmed me.

I could not imagine the fate of the woman unable to have children. *The woman.* In that moment of not-knowing, the heroine of my first novel began to emerge. I did not know her name. I had no knowledge of how she might have lived. And, she was with me. *Find my story,* she said. *Tell it.* Her words echoed in Hotomquam's great silence.

I went in to my bed, a mattress on the floor and a sleeping bag. I lay under the silver glowing in the window and knew I was no longer alone. The question was with me. And, lying ahead, as surely as Scheherazade's thousand and one stories had, the answers shone like stars whose light had yet to reach the earth.

Or candlelight glowing in the windows of a woman no longer mother, no longer lover, no longer anything but trust. A woman being carried by another woman's story toward apprenticeship, toward her life's true work, toward her spirit's home. Toward herself.

# Big Window

■ ■ ■

I saw a hand-lettered flyer on a telephone pole in Flagstaff's old downtown. STOP URANIUM MINING AT THE GRAND CANYON. I went to the first meeting in an old coffee house in the heart of downtown, as I had come toward the unknown Hopi woman's ancient story. A woman carried by a vow.

The mining company engineer, a jolly guy with an abundant gut, flannel shirt, and worn Levi's, told us that when they did the exploratory drilling, *they hadn't seen no animals, hardly none at all.* I'd overheard him before the meeting. His English had been perfect and businesslike. I figured he'd misjudged his audience. He assured us simple country folks that the mine itself was nothing, a breccia pipe deal, the meadow in which it would be sunk no more than fourteen acres. And, THERE WOULD BE JOBS.

After he left, a few of us gathered to begin planning our resistance. A tall guy bent with arthritis said, "Let's go out there. I want to see the place." He nodded to me. "How about you?"

"You know who Ed Abbey is?" I asked.

"Sister," the guy said, "are you ever in the right place!"

I knew I carried a third vow, one unspoken, one distinctly ignoble: to meet the next love of my life. A few weeks into the fight against the uranium mine, I thought I had. He was a brilliant, wiry Deadhead whose perfect fantasy was Stevie Nicks. He was funny and gloomy. Jittery. Incapable of meeting my eyes. Turning away, then taking my hand and saying, "Our brains are running rapids." Jumping up from his chair and heading for the door. "I've got to go. Call you later." He made Mr. Elusive look like an adoring puppy.

I spent two days waiting for a call from the guy, I should have known better. I am not Stevie Nicks. Forty-eight hours of the same old same old, wondering if I shouldn't just pack my bags, go home, and devote my life to gin and missing Nicholas. Clearly, I had dragged my love-junkie self along on my big leap into freedom.

I sat gloomily on my front porch in shorts and a flannel shirt, stretching my legs out to the fine warmth of a late March sun. It was a gorgeous afternoon, the scent of pine pouring down Mars Hill. I managed to be ungrateful in the face of that.

I'd left the door open IN CASE THE PHONE RANG. It didn't. I found myself twisting into the Moebius strip I knew too well, no beginning, no end in sight. I made coffee, drank it, took out my notebook and tried to write away the constriction. The only words that moved from my pen were *I've done it again. Come 2,200 miles to go through the same old same old.*

I tried every pitifully hopeful psychological technique I knew. Write a love letter to the person and burn it. Write a love letter to yourself and mail it. Obsess about the whole mess for half an hour, or till you're bored cross-eyed. All I got was cross-eyed.

I walked out to the sidewalk and looked up at the snow-capped mountains. It seemed blasphemy for my tiny misery to be in the presence of their huge beauty. "Help me," I said. "Help me feel connected—to anything but this bullshit."

The mountains had business of their own. Then, as I muttered a thoroughly ungracious *thanks,* I had a thought. If nothing else, I could go toward beauty. And feed some ravens. That much. I packed water and corn chips and climbed into my Firebird.

I drove the Sunset Crater/Wupatki road toward the ombré violet and rose of the Painted Desert. My heart felt like a lump of sludge. I persisted, made the right turn toward Wukoki ruin, and realized I was crying. Wukoki, as always, shocked me sane, its three broken rooms and tower emerging from a huge sandstone boulder, walls and rock glowing the same blood-orange against the black sand.

I walked to the east side of the ruin, down into a broad wash, between rabbit brush and ephedra, over sand laced with the tracks of lizard and mouse. I turned and faced Wukoki. The fine asymmetry of the old masonry was sharp-edged against the late-afternoon sun, the slope of the sacred mountains just visible beyond the tower. I raised my arms to shadow and light, to the ancient volcanoes, and to the people who had once worked and loved here. My body felt wholly mine, as though blood and muscle and bone were remembering a way to pray I had never been taught.

"I don't even believe in you," I said. "But, I can't do this by myself anymore. If you help me, I will serve you till the day I die."

I remembered that March afternoon long before when a fifteen-year-old Catholic girl believed she had chosen her body over her soul, her pleasure over God. And how I had distrusted sixties gurus, and yet taken the explanations and placebos of psychology as a kind of god-speak. I saw I had worshiped men's desire, had made my stories about them into myths, as though I had been a Scheherazade not so much saving her life, as her soul. I remembered that after Nicholas left, I had ached to believe in something bigger than his huge absence, something much more reliably sheltering than good gin.

"Big Whatever," I said to the huge desert, the huger sky, "I'm here. You better be too."

Nothing happened. There was no brush of an unseen wing against my cheek, no ancient whispers in my ear. All I knew was that it felt good to stretch my arms out to nothing but surrender. It felt good, for the first time in my life, to give up.

I waited. I stopped being smart. And then, the empty window in the eastern wall caught my eye. It was no more than a shadow. Black as the glass chunks in the walls of my new house, dull as the basalt around me. I blinked. The afterimage burned on my retina. And when I looked up, a ghost window shimmered against the sky, as though it were a tiny opening in a great blue window, vast as what I suddenly knew I did not know, a window big as my surrender.

"I'll take what comes next," I said and walked slowly back to my car.

I drove home, picked up homemade tacos at El Charro, and settled in with my journal. Someone knocked on the door. It was not the Stevie Nicks fan. Nor Nicholas magically returned.

A tall blond woman stood on my stoop. She held a pan of warm chocolate chip cookies in one hand. "I'm Diane," she said. "I hope I'm not barging in, but I guessed you're new in town."

"I am," I said. "In my world a chocolate chip cookie is always welcome." An hour later the cookies were gone and we suspected we were sisters, a connection that has held steady to this day. She walked me through my first greenhorn months, told me what guys to watch out for, which tiny restaurant sold their leftovers at half price, and that the black glass in the walls of my home was obsidian, which you could find on the ground a few miles west of town.

I walked her through what is her private story—literally walked. Evening after evening, we hiked in Buffalo Park, on a two-mile-long trail through a big wildflower meadow at the base of the sacred mountains. The curving path became our confes-

sional, our haven, our two-woman treatment center. We have
walked there, in perfect silence, with stumbling words, for eighteen years, but it is an October evening three years into our
friendship I remember best.

We had walked for an hour and were ready to leave. The air
had gone icy. Sunset began to melt blood and bronze beyond
the western edge of the trail. We paused and watched. We could
not leave. She had kids to feed. I had yet another date with my
solitude. A few indigo clouds moved in. The light wove between
them. Copper. Violet. Shell pink.

"Stop," we yelled at the alchemical light. "We can't take any
more."

The light insisted. Altered. Blossomed rose-gold and purple.
For half an hour, an hour, an eternity. We stayed till all that was
left was a thread of pale green. Peridot, light like mineral. And
watching it, their arms around each other, two women shaking
with cold, their hearts filled with sky.

# Animal Time

■ ■ ■

The western sky worked on me. The Big Whatever, which was the closest I could come to naming god/goddess/Pan/Kali/Ma Earth, lived part-time in desert dawn and the last sliver of twilight. That much I knew for sure.

And the more I knew light, the more I knew how little I knew of myself—my animal self, the inner ebbs and flows of blood and spirit that responded not to clocks but to the immutable shifts of sun and moon. I understood that in disconnecting from pain, I had also removed myself from my deepest knowledge. In running toward the shelter of men's arms, I had fled the greater haven. And in my frantic busyness, had outrun the heartbeat of the earth.

The moon jolted me awake—more precisely, the absence of moon. I had been offered a little rental south of town, a one-room cabin in a cluster of other cabins in an old resort. There was no running water, no central heat. A woodstove sat in the middle of the living-bed-dining-room. There was electricity, and a weather-beaten shower house a few hundred feet away. The cabin and its surrounding meadow and pine forest seemed like wilderness. Vast. Harboring the possibility of bears, the assurance of silence. One more step toward nowhere to run.

I called the owner. "I'll take it." *I'm scared. I'll do it.*

I moved in late summer. The first evening I stepped out of

my cabin to walk to the shower, I carried a flashlight, a whistle, and a can of bear spray for the fifty-yard journey. Sunset burned rose-gold. The full moon drifted beyond the dark pines. I stood alone in the clearing, tilted my face to rose light, then silver. I tucked the whistle in my bathrobe pocket and put out the flashlight.

The next night I walked out at the same time. No flashlight. No whistle. No bear spray. The sun glowed molten. The eastern sky cooled and went dark. I waited for the moon. And waited. I wondered if I had stepped into a twist in time. Or finally gone crazy.

At last the moon rose. My landlord came out of his cabin.

"The moon was late," I said.

He laughed gently. "No," he said. "It's right on time. You've been in cities for too long."

I wondered *where* I had been through all my Northeastern nights, blind, perhaps—and how an intelligent woman with a background in laboratory science had seen so little. I began to rise with the sun and watch through sunset. I'd wait to put on lights in my cabin, let the place grow cool blue, then gray, then dark. I felt the days shrink, the nights begin to stretch out. I felt my spirits lift as sun broke free from monsoon clouds. I understood how the gray light of my eastern home had dragged me down, how the western light was changing the cellular structure of my body. Transmuting my inner clock into a keeper of Animal Time.

Animal Time. What geese know, and lizards, and my own species long, long ago.

# Dead Bill

■ ■ ■

I began to live more fully in Animal Time, to wake, eat, and sleep by the wisdom of my body. It was late spring, then early summer. I wondered how I had ever lived in any other way. As I returned to the knowledge of my cells, the disconnection of too much alcohol no longer felt magical, the hangovers felt toxic. I stopped drinking. And wondered why I had ever started.

I found myself able to sit quietly for hours, watching light change, ignoring the phone, learning just how long it takes a horned toad to find its way from the two-trunked ponderosa to the poppies. I found myself listening to music without disconnecting into nostalgia. I remembered how much I loved the hook. I played the old blues and danced alone.

And then one July twilight, Animal Time took me farther. I wasn't hunting male shelter. I figured it would be pointless because I'd had a perm that afternoon and still smelled like ammonia. I pulled on a loose cotton dress, slid my feet into ugly-but-comfortable sandals, and headed for Monsoon's, an old downtown bar. The point was not to score. The point was to dance. Tommy Dukes was playing the blues.

It was a long, soft evening, a train howling by, the street glittery with new pickups down from the Rez and low riders over from the South Side. I stood outside the bar watching sunset fade to indigo over Mars Hill, opened the door, and walked into a room full of smoke, strangers, and screaming guitar. Dukes slammed into "Messin' with the Kid." I ordered a lime and soda and moved alone onto the dance floor. His voice was a blade in my blood and I was cut loose. A gone girl.

I danced by myself for a couple numbers totally content. A college boy asked me to dance. I did. Might just as well have been boogying alone. A big bearded guy with a full glass in his hand walked up.

"You mind if I dance with your lady?" he asked the kid.

"The lady decides for herself," I said.

"How about it?" the guy said. "I like your attitude."

I looked up into a big grin and warm gray eyes and said, "Why not?"

Dukes and the boys burned into Chuck Willis's "Feel So Bad." I felt so good, even though I could have been dancing with a slightly loaded and highly enthusiastic bear. When the band moved into "Born Under a Bad Sign," the bear put its arms around me and I stepped back.

"Actually," I said, "I haven't been this close to a guy in a long time."

The bear laughed. "Me either. I mean a woman. Let's see what happens."

He put his arms around me and I breathed in the scent of Nicholas. Heat. Woodsmoke. The smell of a hardworking man fresh out of the shower. I knew I was in trouble. And as he buried his face in my hair and said, "I can already tell you're a real woman," I figured the trouble would be happening on pure Animal Time. It would be the farthest thing from shelter. I could hardly wait for it to start.

The bear's name was Bill. Was. He's been dead six years now. Dead Bill had once, in I Corps near Da Nang, been nicknamed Bear. He'd been a special forces medic going in for extractions in Laos when our American soldiers were not in Laos. But in

1985, Bill was in the heart of my new heaven on earth and he was about as alive as any man I'd known for a long time. He became my guide into Southwestern wildness, a wildness as raw and gorgeous as what we shaped with our desire. White water. Hot springs. Monsoons.

We drove out two-track roads that were more like gullies, hiked on mountain and canyon switchback, along three-hundred-foot drop-offs. He rowed the Green River through Desolation and Gray Canyons while I clung to the rigging and counted myself lucky to be scared wordless.

Our Southwestern wildness is now gone as thoroughly as Bill himself, because it was not just blue Utah canyon shadows and burnt orange hoodoo rocks; or lightning flashing over the slick rock on which, by virtue of lust and folly, we had no choice but to wait out the storm; or class 5 rapids that could corkscrew you into a conversation with your mortality. What we found in what we and our friends called "back of the beyond" were small towns with thin Mormon coffee, lousy food, dusty old hardware stores, a gloomy café run by an old, old woman rumored to have killed her husband, motels that wouldn't let you check in without a ring on the lady's finger, stories, stories, a writer's life worth of stories.

Too much of this fine human messiness is gone now, except for my memories of the tight-lipped couple guiding their five kids away from the drunk couple giggling their way toward the Flamingo Motel; the bright pink tag on the key to Room 104 and the way the sagging mattress squeaked as Bill and I fell onto the bed, not bothering to close the door, nor taking off any more clothes than necessary.

Bill was on his way to the next warm body by early winter '85, his parting words: "I just don't have those stars in my eyes. Besides, sooner or later, I'll cheat on you. I always do." What he left in his wake, what I found in his wake, was a deepening of my growing love affair with a Western earth even bigger than desire. And knowledge I didn't know I'd learned till I found myself using it alone: how to pick campsites, pack what I needed, and not make lame excuses when I hadn't.

Bill and I would come apart, reconnect, and come apart three more times between 1985 and 1993, the last time forever, as he lied his way into an affair with a woman who had been my friend. He died without us saying good-bye on the evening of my fifty-sixth birthday.

The morning after I heard about his death, I made myself remember with affection how we had run the San Juan River, the Verde, and, for eighteen days of fierce luminosity, the Colorado River. I thanked his ghost for loaning me his inflatable kayak, in which I paddled the San Juan by myself during a full eclipse of the sun, watching pale green willows cast long shadows, wondering what the probability of being a woman paddling a red desert river in the quartz light of an eclipse noon would be. I knew his gifts had been white water, the loan of the little boat, and the lesson, yet again, that a faithless guy is a faithless guy.

It wasn't until 2000, four years after his death, that I finally cried. The circle closed. In a way predictably cruel and oddly graceful. I had gone to our used bookstore, looking for an old copy of Orson Scott Card's *A Planet Called Treason*. I found instead Terry Tempest Williams's *Desert Quartet*, sat down on the floor, and began to read. Her words carried me into a slot canyon, let me keep company with a woman moving over the desert alone.

The bookstore manager found me lost in plunge pools and blades of light. "I've got your old novel," he said and handed me two copies of *Sisters of the Dream*. I opened the first book. It was inscribed: *For Bill, with love, friendship and amends. (heart) Mary P.S. It's just fiction. December 25, 1992.*

I pulled myself to my feet and leaned on the shelf of Southwest Americana, breathless, as though the mean past had just sucker-punched me in the gut. Southwest Americana, the indie tune on the store speakers, Matt, the sweetly fuzzy clerk who had handed me the book and was looking at me with concern—everything seemed dreamlike and hyperreal.

I didn't want to see what I held in my hands, the book I gave Dead Bill when he was extraordinarily Live Bill and we were lovers. I had heard that my former dear friend for whom Dead Bill had left me was moving out of town with her new husband. I imagined her briskly separating things into piles. *Keep. Get rid of.* Much as she had once sorted through our friendship.

I made myself occupy exactly where and who I was. "Thanks," I said to Matt in what I hoped was a normal voice. I put *Desert Quartet* and the two copies of *Sisters of the Dream* in my shopping basket, paid, and walked slowly out into early evening. Each step, each breath required careful thought. As though I had left my body behind. In the bookstore, at the instant I opened the book. In my living room, as a woman's voice years earlier told me Bill was dead. I knew there were tears on my cheeks only because they were warmer than the twilight air.

Back home, I opened Dead Bill's former book out on my desk. For an instant I wanted to tear out the dedication and burn it. I would pray the smoke drifted south and blinded my former dear friend at some critical moment in her driving out of town.

Instead I drew a line through *For Bill* and wrote above the canceled words: *For My Own Heart.* It didn't mend a thing—until now.

# Minimum Wage

■ ■ ■

The first twelve years of my life in the Southwest now seem as perfectly woven as a Hopi bride's marriage robe. A male relative does the weaving. The cloth is off-white, the color of winter clouds over the peaks. There is a border of red dashes. For a woman's lifeblood.

I wove my blood into those early years, and my passion. Passion for the vast light. For writing the shape of the generous earth beneath my feet. Passion for gathering stories. And writing them. Passion for radical activism. Passion for doing what I had left undone.

My friend Roxane reminds me often that "radical" springs from the Latin for "root." I took root here. Not with epiphanies. Nor with adventures. I took root as I had once buried my hands in the rich dirt of my Northeast garden. Weaving myself, as roots do, into the soil. The Havasupai tribe, my friends in Canyon Under Siege, and I held off the Canyon uranium mine for four years, just long enough for the price of uranium to plummet. Looking back, that battle seems a gift. I remember my coworker Dan Daggett looking out over the scarred mine site and saying, "Someday we're going to wish all we had to fight was mines and logging." I asked him what he meant. "Development," he said quietly, "and off-road vehicles chewing up everything."

Bill ambled in and out of my life. I met other men, but compared to his big vitality, they were shadows. Disappointments. Despite my joy in Animal Time, I caught myself too often in search of that old shelter—and the men I met confused *me* with shelter. Their bad luck.

Though it had been easy to stop drinking, my jones for the boy that doesn't call was relentless. In 1987 a woman friend took me to a twelve-step meeting. I sat down wondering what I was doing in a smoky room with a bunch of old guys who seemed to be talking about nothing but the great times they used to have, and God. Big *G* God. The God that noticed every time a woman got on a horse for fun. I started to leave.

Then the not-so-old guy at the end of the table said, "I was raised with a God that hated horny little boys. That kept me out of these rooms for thirty years. One January morning I woke up half-dead in the alley behind Monsoon's and I fired that God."

I took off my backpack, grabbed a cup of truly bad coffee, and sat down to listen.

I learned. About how little I knew, and that it was time for me to turn healing over to the Big Healer. It was time to remember my therapist's hands on my shoulders and her words, "Stop being so quick for five minutes." It was time to slow down, to do plain work. Work with my hands. Work that didn't try to make the mysterious mundane.

I worked for a few years as cook and baker at Macy's, the little café in which I'd eaten my first meal. Hands-on work. Shaping soup buns, swirling cream-cheese frosting into dark brownies, chopping peppers and mushrooms for a hippie Vietnamese soup. Mindful work, with just enough room for stories to begin to form.

I earned four bucks an hour, a tenth of what I'd made back east. There were no benefits except for more whipped cream and chocolate than even I could eat. I felt rich, privileged, a woman lucky to be exactly who she was. So it was a shock the morning the woman in the fur coat came barreling up to the coffee counter. I was writing on the menu board next to the pastry case: *posole, Parmesan-spinach buns, red pepper and Jack cheese quiche.* My hair was tied back in a knot. I wore a smeared apron over Levi's and a floppy T-shirt. The woman slammed me into the wall.

I turned and saw her face. Perfectly made-up. Jaw set. She said not one word of apology, or of recognition she might have hurt me. I wondered where she had come from. I hoped she would go back. Had I known she was a ghost from the future—my future, Flagstaff's future, the future of the West—I would have taken her by the arm, turned her to face me, and said, "There's nothing for you here." But back then I had no idea. Few of us did.

I'm grateful for that innocence. Between 1985 and 1997, I was given a lifetime of believing I had been reborn into writing and friendship and a region so hugely magical it seemed eternal. I thought I had finally come to immutable shelter.

Imagine. The heart is on a road trip. I drive up a dirt road in one-hundred-degree Nevada heat, park, sleep-walk a few hundred yards into a canyon, and stand under a waterfall, watching spray glitter like stars.

Imagine. The heart is white water. A river grabs our boat. We go down. It seems forever. I am held by something other than water, pure blue-green—and I am released into fearing nothing.

Imagine. The heart is quiet. I stand in the hollow of a slick rock arch. There are cobalt mountains against last light. Pale birds seem to fly in and out of the rising moon. I have no thoughts. Not one.

Summer 1987 gleams in recollection like a necklace of days perfect as the ancient beads the lucky sometimes find in a hidden wash: dawns subtle as jasper, midnights bright as the obsidian that filled my new home. I'd moved into a larger cabin, the one I occupy now. Each morning I hauled my old blue rocker to the back deck, drank my morning coffee, watched the tips of the dark trees go silver, then pale pink. I wrote and edited there, and after a day as satisfying as a good meal or good loving, watched last light fade beyond the trees.

Each night I lay awake, as a child does on Xmas Eve, barely able to fall asleep with excitement over morning coming. Not because of a new lover. But because Talasi, the heroine of my book, had become Scheherazade. She told her stories through my fingers on my electric typewriter, and when she fell silent, I walked out on the dirt road into the pine trees, trusting that when I returned to the writing, she would be waiting. She always was.

I had not imagined this work, my real work, would be so easy. My days were simple. No man. No alcohol. I woke to coffee and light, wrote till eleven-thirty, went to a support meeting where there was just enough talk, just enough silence. I came home, wrote more, drove up to Buffalo Park, and walked three to four miles on the curving trail at the base of the Sacred Mountains— heading west out of my good day, then back east into my unknown evening. Sometimes Diane walked with me. Sometimes I walked alone.

One twilight I was stopped in my solitary tracks by a huge silver globe drifting up away from the mountainside. I wondered if the Harmonic Convergers had been right. I thought about making a confession and realized I had nothing to confess. The globe moved up and away from the mountain. Full moon. I raised my arms and prayed only for one thing: the possibility of amazement for the rest of my life.

My prayers seemed to be answered in the most routine and amazing way. I worked at the café day after day, made a hundred red-pepper quiches, a thousand cream-cheese brownies, folded the same handfuls of chocolate chips into the same tubs of batter. I walked with Diane on the Buffalo Park trail a hun-

dred times. I faced into the blank piece of paper in my typewriter, and knowing nothing, found Talasi's story scrolling out,
morning after morning after morning. I ate almost the same
thing every night. Linguine, garlic, olive oil, good Parmesan,
and fresh broccoli; or homemade chicken fried rice. Ritual
food. Exactly enough. After dinner I sat in what was left of the
light, in the company of the greatest happiness I had ever
known, and waited for what came next.

# CRACK IN THE WORLD

# Ev

■ ■ ■

It was during that summer of ordinary joy that I met another wiry red-haired guy—at a Grand Canyon anti–uranium mining demonstration. He pulled to the side of the road, took a flyer from my hand, and said, "What are you guys doing?"

I told him. He climbed out of the truck, grabbed a handful of flyers, and stood next to me. He said he was from New York. On his way to no longer being from New York. No job. No safety net. Just fire for the West. Did I know what he was talking about?

"You ever read Ed Abbey?" I said.

He pulled a copy of *The Monkey Wrench Gang* from his backpack.

"Man," I said, "are you ever in the right place."

We kept talking. We haven't stopped, talking our way up talus slopes under white-hot Mohave sun, into a bend in a slot canyon no wider than our shoulders, down the crumbling face of a mesa we should never have crawled up. And we talked ourselves into friendship. Hard friendship. Easy as sliding into the current in the slow San Juan and floating to the next eddy.

We have never been lovers. Great good luck.

Ev came back west in the early nineties on a vacation, then, as I had, came back for good. To work as a waiter at the Grand Canyon, spending every minute away from his job exploring, moving on canyon trails as Scheherazade once told stories.

In 1995 he moved into the cabin next door. It was the perfect not-marriage. Good coffee and better talk on my back stoop. Nickel-and-dime gourmet for dinner and world-class Scrabble and more talk. No topic was taboo. Proximity granted us the minutiae of intimacy. Separate cabins granted us oceans of space.

As I think about the early days of our friendship, I see travertine, depositions of truth, carried by intentions fluid and hidden as underground rivers. There are pockets of treasures, the astonishment of discovering we both loved hard trails, Luther Allison, Forty-Second and Broadway in the early seventies, mean slot machines, and generous casino buffets.

We talked about what would happen when he found a lover. He wanted one. I didn't. I taught him my favorite saying: *Don't take your present hostage for some hypothetical future.*

He taught me the words I had decided never again to say: "I'm not leaving this friendship."

We taught each other the peril of Yuppie crises. He'd rolled into town from a two-week pack trip straight to Macy's. I met him there. We were agonizing over whether to split a cranberry twist and a sticky bun, or go for linguine and Alfredo sauce. He wanted sugar. I wanted fat. I felt my jaw tighten, saw his forehead corrugate. "Oh, my God," I said, "it's a Yuppie crisis."

We drove away from each other on solo road trips, brought back stories, set them out between us as though they were bones or geodes or broken survey stakes. Hot springs on the bank of a frozen river. Slaughtered mountain lion carcasses stinking in a wash. Little towns suddenly doubled in size, and old downtowns gone boutique. More and more, our talk turned to outrage. And we agreed, if nothing else, to bear witness. We did. Watching and taking field notes on the greatest dislocation either of us had ever known.

One evening we drove home from rock climbing at dusk. The scent of pine seemed stronger than ever. As we turned off old Route 66, we saw, where there had been a hundred acres of forest, dozers and stumps and a sign that said THE PINES AT THE MOUNTAIN. AFFORDABLE LUXURY. SOUTHWEST CONDOMINIUM LIVING.

Ev waved at the clear-cuts. "The pines? Where?"

The neighborhood had begun to go bad a few years earlier. The forest slopes, their limestone outcroppings, lupine, and gambel oak, their perfect habitat for owl, coyote, and hapless rabbit had been Frankensteined into a Wal-Mart strip mall. A few people had fought the development, but the city council had been assured Wal-Mart would landscape. They did. With southern pines that died on the spot.

"Affordable luxury?" Ev said.

"Oxymoron," I said.

We high-fived.

Wealthy immigrants began to pour in. I thought of Tibet. Of the Chinese occupation. Of how too many of us devour what we think we love.

One spring evening Ev and I went to hear the sacred music of the Gaden Shartse Tibetan Buddhist monks. Their small human throats chanted the sound of mountains. The Snow Lion danced on his four human feet, his huge grin reminding us that breath is joy. The young exiled Tibetan monk told us in five minutes all we would ever need to know about homesickness. I felt how tiny my losses were, glanced at Ev.

"Time to get over Yuppie crises," I whispered.

"What are we becoming?" he said.

Too many of the audience wore blissfully opaque smiles. Too many of them wore Nouveau Oestern: stone-washed denim head to toe, pounds of silver and turquoise around every visible appendage, immaculate Tony Lama cowperson boots.

"Let's wait," I said, "till everybody leaves. I want to see what this audience puts in the donation box."

"Yeah," he said. "Let's see the true value of compassion."

There was fifteen dollars in the big plastic box. In ones and fives.

We watched. We didn't want to see. Somebody was projecting a bad movie on the screen of the Southwest. Ev and I would mourn another wetland gone, another canyon gutted for a golf course, and after there was nothing left to say, we would shrug. "But nobody's shooting at us," one of us would say.

*We* were not under attack. We were not Jews in Nazi Germany, guys walking point near Da Nang, Tibetans watching our homes shelled to rubble. What was dying were alligator junipers and deer mice and hawks, and the web that held them perfectly connected. I had yet to fully understand what the molecular physicists know: we are all one.

And then Ev told me he would spend the summer in the Wind River Mountains in Wyoming. A thousand miles or more north.

I nodded. "Sounds perfect for you," I said. After all, what are friends for? And I thought it would be easy to just slide back into my gorgeous solitude. Dead Bill's double departure had taught me how to say good-bye. Easy. You don't.

# Deathwatch

■ ■ ■

The West began to be colonized by nightmares that were all too real. It was not the first time. Ask the Hopi. Ask the Havasupai and Tohono O'odham. Ask what lies under the Goldwater Bombing Range, what lies under Anthem's "master-planned" development; ask the residents of the desert town New River next door. Ask the cholla. The luna moth. The desert bighorn. The ubiquitous horned toad, which each day becomes less and less ubiquitous.

I remember feeling as though I had been asleep on my feet, not paying heed, and awakened trapped, as one faux-wakes into a bad dream and begins the efforts to escape, again and again, to find oneself always in the same place. Trapped in déjà vu.

The carving up of the West began to seem as great a mutilation as the change in my mother as she descended into psychosis. Her eyes would glitter or go flat, her mouth narrow to a tight line. Her voice would become the voice of a child or a dying woman. She would seem to shrivel into herself. Just before it seemed she would disappear, the ambulance would come and she would be gone.

Time would slow. Lose meaning. And then my mother would return, her face gray, hands trembling. She reeked of the medicine they gave her to sleep. Her wit was dulled, her fine sarcasm gone. Her fingers on her beloved piano keys were clumsy.

Slowly, slowly, she would resume her normal shape, the shape of a mother. But after the third episode, I knew normal shape was only temporary, and contained something nameless that would overpower my mother and leave behind a zombie.

Consider the desert as mother. Cholla and saguaro are scraped away, the land buried under an outlet mall. The wild meadow is turned into a golf course. There is talk of indigenous landscaping, the use of recycled water. But the truth lies in the words of a local developer, whose cheery green-spin I once endured: *First we nuke it, then we mitigate.*

I had none of this knowledge as I slowly came awake to what was happening—except I knew it was not the first time I had faced dislocation. I made myself remember. My hometown, Irondequoit, New York, gone, its cantaloupe farms and peach orchards bulldozed for suburbs, its low hills and glittering creeks leveled and filled for shopping centers. Rochester's inner city, which had been reclaimed by hippies and neighborhood folks after the white flight to the suburbs, became the charming trophy of stock market bottom feeders and MBAs. And now, here, signs that read AFFORDABLE LUXURY.

I was foggy with wanting to not know, yet I made myself write. I told myself bearing witness might matter. Here is one of my first field notes in *Unnatural History:*

---

*2/11/1997: I'm working a weekend gig in Phoenix. I sit in the shade of alien palm trees. They were brought to this hotel court-yard forty years ago by an entrepreneur who figured a snazzy motel in the desert ought to be named Safari and, given that, have palm trees.*

*The pool is Martian blue; the birds are gypsy cowbirds who've flapped in from who knows where—and are taking over the neighborhood. They lay their eggs in Inca doves' nests. The duped mama dove raises her huge foster baby as her own, aston-*

*ished at its greed, frantic to gather enough to fill its yawping mouth.*

*Alien birds in alien trees in a city so alien the air seems more dangerous than the atmosphere of another planet.*

*I too am alien. I come down from the northern Arizona mountains. I walk for hours on these long shadow streets. Last night I went into a sports bar and it was* Star Wars. *Six television screens on which mutantly tall men throw basketballs into hoops, again and again, replays shimmering under black light; the disco howling from the speakers was early Donna Summers. It could have been 1976. It could have been the mutable future. I could have been anywhere.*

I had believed Flagstaff was exempt. By virtue of its redneck grit, its knife-sharp mountain winters, its downtown bars with boards over the windows because there's no point in replacing broken glass that will just get broken again by a flying bottle— or body. I was wrong.

I collected my field notes in a little gray notebook with *Deathwatch* scrawled across the cover. Its pages became a file of the petty crimes of the new arrivés. I remember the late-middle-aged man I waited behind in Macy's Café. He wore a thousand dollars' worth of shorts and shirt, Missoni sweater, boots, pager, watch, and bad haircut. His "Where's my refill?" to the busy counter kid was not a question. He picked up a food co-op flyer and said, "Co-op, Jesus Christ. Why should the rich share what they have? What are *they* doing wrong?"

I wondered if somebody really was making a movie. The guy's words were too pat, too clichéd, too much proof of Ev's and my suspicions. The signs were everywhere. Huge SUVs raced sixty miles an hour on our downtown streets. Nobody's turn signal worked. There was the woman who came shrieking into the bookstore because she'd broken her fingernail and "Oh, my

God, where's there a nail salon, because my hubby and I are from out of town and I don't know where *anything* is?"

I began to transform my field notes into essays. I wanted to take raw pain to other eyes and hearts. Maybe I'd find kin. Maybe I'd alert the rich 'n' rude to the fact that they were not envied. They were held in contempt. They didn't need the gates on their enclaves. Most of the rest of us didn't want in.

Sometime during the Deathwatch, I'm not sure when, I lost ninety dollars at the Apache casino. I slid ninety dollars I didn't have—a ten-dollar bill at a time—into a slot machine. I played till three A.M., drove up the fifty-mile-long hill from the casino to Flagstaff through country that abounds with highway-crazed elk, on a highway glazed with black ice. Ice you cannot see. Ice that will spin you into your death faster than it takes ten dollars, played eighteen nickel credits at a time, to disappear into a slot machine. I remember my hands clenched on the steering wheel, and the slightly shocky whirl of my thoughts: At least the money goes to Indians. At least it's reparation.

I was sick of loss that was not reparation. Attrition in the meadows and badlands, attrition in my heart. I'd seen the death of my dad, my mom, two dear friends—and Bill. Diane and I had drifted apart. Two of my sons were in Asia, my daughter and granddaughter across the country in the Northeast. I looked at my face in the mirror and saw a woman well on her way to being old. Looked at the Old West and saw it eaten by the New.

I had forgotten my prayer at Wukoki. For connection. For deep connection with the earth. I had forgotten that true connection, like true affection, is most assuredly for better and for worse.

Somehow, I kept faith. Day after day, morning, afternoon, and twilight, wild weather or tame, I took myself to a little cluster of seven pines just off our dirt road. I sat on the pine needle duff soft in their heart. I fed the ravens who lived there, learned they far preferred old French-fried onion rings to blue corn. I paid attention to the hundred teachers of the place. The owl that left its pellets filled with mice bones. The cranesbill geraniums that bloomed no bigger than my baby fingernail in dark patches of first snowmelt. The maggots that fed on the fawn carcass left by poachers. The last rays of sun in the fawn's rib cage. The little body shining like a lantern.

I held my hands out to light and shadow, saw the wrinkles, saw the veins running blue beneath my skin. I understood that my cells would someday be food and drink, my bones no more than armature. I began to know, without question, that every cell in my body, every thought, every feeling in my spirit, existed only because of the earth around me. I was Earth, Air, Fire, and Water. No more, no less. This knowledge was not metaphor, it was pure physics. The earth, in the deepest sense, was my mother.

Finally, one slow twilight, after I'd raged because the prairie dog colony at the southern gateway to town was to be relocated to make room for a new chain motel, I sat in the heart of the trees and said, "Thank you. I get it." My long-ago prayer at Wukoki had been answered. Connection.

I took in what I saw outside. In the mirror I took in my aging. I had promised myself since I was a young woman working with old women nursing-home patients that I would never disguise how time moved in me. The vow was easy when I was twenty.

At fifty-seven, I saw life eating me. My body. My face. I had made the decision to move through menopause in Animal Time—without estrogen. I wanted to be the aging woman I had come this far to be.

I had stopped bleeding in 1995, but the waning of my hormones seemed to take forever. Too often I felt as though I had a persistent first-degree burn of the emotions. Glare and loud noise flooded me. I couldn't not see what I saw. I wondered if the horror stories of "change of life" were simply stories told by women who finally saw the truth.

I learned the rhythm of the hot flashes. I realized that as they flooded me, they washed away anxiety and confusion. I began to bless them, and I blessed my work, which did not require panty hose, or any business suit but a loose shirt and pants. I blessed our cool mountain nights, and the way Buffalo Park's trail would stretch out in front of me, promising at its end that I would feel, if not happy, a little more peaceful. I blessed other women who wrote about menopause and assured me I would make it through.

And I began to understand that the aging face I saw in my mirror was the same face seen by half the world—that is, by men. That is, *not* seen. I began to face into what that meant.

*3/5/1997: I think of K. dancing across the rock gym floor, her black velvet hat pulled down to her dark eyebrows, her strong legs and feet carrying her no less gracefully than a young doe's. We were listening to Junior Wells and K. was shimmying, undulating, trailing a brilliant red scarf through the air, around her young breasts, across her narrow hips.*

*I watched her. I watched the men watching her. I loved what she was and I wanted to crouch in a corner and howl into my cupped hands, "That was me. That was once me."*

*I could have stepped out to join her. I might have matched her step for step, move for move. A dancer always dances. But the red scarf was not mine. A black one, perhaps, maybe gray. There would be no point in trailing it across my sagging breasts, around my still-narrow hips, no point in letting it pour, silken and seductive, down the long line of my leg.*

*I watched K. dance. I didn't move. Or speak. Or breathe my sorrow out in one long breath, a sigh of black silk I would gather from the air and tie around my aging body.*

# Crack in the World

■ ■ ■

L. Q. Navarro used to say there are two Americas. . . . One bunch wants good things for the world. The other bunch thinks the earth is there to be ground up for profit.

—JAMES LEE BURKE,
*Bitterroot*

The world cracked open, not with the slow grace of cranesbill geraniums pushing up through the forest floor, nor with the thunderclap of tons of orange rock spalling away from a sandstone mesa. It was mid-April in 1997. Ev was gone, scouting the ranger job in the Wind River Mountains in Wyoming. He was often out of phone contact. There was no question he would spend the summer there. It was unsettling not to have him next door, not be able to babble some random thought, some great wisdom. I began to realize what a gift he was, and I to him. The generosity of our connection was new to me. How we never apologized; we rarely explained.

I thought I would be fine with his absence—until he was gone. Perhaps I would have found our separation less painful if I hadn't continued to see what was happening to the West, and felt alone with the knowledge. I know now that others saw and felt the same, wondering if they were crazy, if they were making a big deal out of ordinary progress. But at that time all I seemed to find were nice people who talked about how important it is to respect different viewpoints, who told me to remember humans are a temporary species and the earth would survive us. Had Ev said those words, it would have been satire.

I remembered the civil rights battle of my youth. Remembered the nice people who once told me they knew some perfectly fine Negroes, but wondered if the Southern colored were capable of thinking for themselves. I saw the earth being treated with similar condescension, or with the malice invading Europeans brought to the native people centuries ago. I couldn't understand why my Flagstaff neighbors, people who hiked Western trails, climbed Western rock, ran desert rivers, and claimed to love this Western land, were not fighting back.

Without Ev's conspiratorial grin, our high fives, the way he stormed into my cabin with the latest newspaper story of developer atrocity, I had no touchstone. I was deeply, subliminally lonely. At the time I would not have told you this was so. I did not believe I needed any human being. I had needed Nicholas and that had nearly killed me. Light, limestone, and the ever faithful casinos would do me just fine.

I began to gamble more and more, submerging in the gorgeous disconnection of the forty-minute drive down out of the pine forest to the Apache casino, to lose myself in the smoky air and glittering lights, in the bright mandalas spinning on the slot machines. I found myself going once a week, then twice, staying five hours, staying eight, driving back up the midnight hill past blurred shadows that could have been elk moving toward the highway. Even the drive itself seemed a wager, my life at stake.

I loved it. Playing slot machines was more perfect than Irish coffee. A win rocketed my adrenaline. The whirling moons, orchids, and pyramids calmed my jittery heart. I stumbled into my cabin and fell asleep with the echoes of jackpot bells my lullaby. Whether Ev came back, whether I would be alone for the rest of my life, I had this.

I don't know what would have happened had the earth not cracked me open. I suspect I might have disappeared into the casinos. Slowly. Steadily. And one day come awake to see my ancient face in the ladies' room mirror, to understand that I had squandered what was left of my life.

I was spared that fate. Not in a light-drenched epiphany, but with a sucker punch that took my breath away. My friend Lottie and I had taken her two dogs for a Sunday walk. We headed for the little valley the locals called the Meadow. We slogged across wet duff to the greening berm of a little tank, where the old dog took a drink and the young one panted happily in the sun, his fur the pure gold of fire agate.

We four walked the fence line. For the first time in months, I felt a little peaceful. I thought about the sanctuary of trees, and of silence. I was grateful that the Meadow was broad, rocky, and free from anything human except broken arrowheads, shards, and old rusted nails. Three, maybe four big old ponderosa lived there. Limestone outcroppings glittered on the long slopes that poured, easy as breath, down from the ridgelines, where more ponderosa grew, and gambel oak, and dwarf wildflowers. I hoped the snowmelt stream that snaked across the Meadow would still be running.

Lottie stopped dead. "No," she whispered. She raised her arm and pointed. I looked out.

The survey stakes were tagged Day-Glo pink. They glowed against the dark trees, and on a forest floor starred with wild geranium and patches of late snow. The tags seemed alien and foreboding as splotches on a mammogram.

"I knew it," my friend said. "I have a gene for finding survey stakes."

A day later my landlord told me what was happening. The

directors of the only gated development in Flagstaff, a place whose golf course destroyed half of Griffith's Spring Canyon and choked off Lindberg Spring, had decided to buy the Meadow and its surrounding ridges. A Phoenix developer would build a second gated golf-course development there, perhaps a hundred yards from the original.

I looked at my landlord, who is my friend. I could not speak. He punched me gently on the arm. "I'm sorry, girl," he said, this guy who lives as far to the right as I do to the left, "they're like roaches. They're all over the West. Haven't you noticed?"

I remember walking back into the cabin as though I moved through the dense air of a bad dream. I knew I was not dreaming. I wanted to run. And I suspected there was nowhere to run, and that I had asked for something, for a connection I had not fully understood. Ev had once told me a few words of Thomas Berry's: *Some of us are nerve endings for the earth.*

I called his voice mail. There was to be an eclipse that night. A full moon rising, Hale-Bopp comet cruising along the western horizon. I told him about the Meadow, said I would pretend he was looking at the same moon, maybe whispering the same prayer. "I hate being a nerve ending," I said. "I hate it."

A week later I invited other friends for brunch. They arrived while my landlord burned slash. Clouds softened the spring light. There were orange fires in the dark trees and the shadows of men tending the flames.

My friends and I set up our table in the west, watched smoke drift toward us and away, again and again. We ate corn bread and melon and real eggs, their yolks dark gold. They had brought a bowl of green apples, honeydew melon, and kiwi. The fruit was chunks of peridot and jade in the shifting light. They brought flowers, golden mums and spotted lilies. Their children hung a dartboard from a young pine.

We finished eating, drained the last cold coffee from our

mugs. Laverne, a Gila River tribal poet, leaned back in his chair. We'd been talking about the Meadow. I told them about my childhood home, how the hills and creek valleys were leveled, how I can't go back to where I comforted my scared self with bright October leaves and crystal-black water running wild over boulders no bigger than my ten-year-old fist.

"When I was eleven," Laverne said, "my dad signed papers and the BIA took me away to school." He looked away.

"Tell her," Chris said, "tell her about the Gila River."

Laverne shook his head like a man shaking off pain. "There were huge cottonwoods and beautiful shadows. Now if you go there, you see nothing but dead sticks along the dead shore."

Without more words, we cleared the table. Molly, Laverne's wife, called in the kids to help. They whispered something to her. "The kids want to go there," she said. "To the Meadow. What do you think?"

"I'd love it," I said. I carried butter and orange juice into the cabin, scattered corn-bread crumbs for the nagging ravens. My friends gathered in a circle to wait. They were laughing. The little boy clung to his dad's leg. I would see that shape of us, again and again, as we walked out to the Meadow together, no one alone, always someone leaning in to talk, someone leaning in to listen.

We came slowly down the long northern slope. The kids gathered sparkly rocks, hoped there would be water, maybe turtles, maybe frogs. Their voices stopped as we came through the trees into the Meadow. There was no one there. The red earth was gouged. There was new equipment at the drill site and a huge plastic-lined hole filled with oily water. "Diamond drill," Laverne said. "They go down, have to clean out the muck." He waved at the oil pond near the drill. "You have to have water to drill, mix it with dirt, mud is the lubricant."

I picked up a plastic soda cup, stuck it in a pipe, looked at the filthy water, and longed to believe in magic, to believe that a woman could plug a drilling pipe with a plastic cup, and stop time.

"I wish I'd brought my sweet grass," Laverne said. "The least we could do is give some smoke for prayer." He shook his head and put his arms around Molly. They pulled me into a hug. We breathed together, as though we *were* sweet-grass smoke.

# Razor Vision

■ ■ ■

*May 1997: Lottie calls me. Her voice is shaking. She tells me she found a pile of beer cans in the forest near her home and then— she cannot believe this—four porn photos tacked to a pine. The shots are of women, and they have been doubly shot, once by the photographer, the second time by whoever tossed the beer cans and pulled the trigger of a .22. I believe this. I remember Dead Bill telling me how the grunts just loved to shoot out the breasts on the Raquel Welch posters.*

*"I can't stand it," she says. "Those holes in the women's bodies, like those survey tags in the Meadow. I couldn't not look at them. They consumed my attention, they consumed everything."*

*She drives over. We sit on my back porch. We are silent, and then we tie bracelets on each other's wrists. I have made the bracelets from red and black thread and one skull bead. We tie four knots, one for each direction: "North," I say, "for the guidance of the Old Ones. East, for the Light. South, for the consuming fires of summer. West, to Our Lady Who Eats That Which Destroys Balance."*

*My friend moves more slowly than I. She is young, perhaps less in shock, perhaps more in pain.*

*"East," she says, "for clear vision. North, for crystal-clear vision. West, for death and night vision. South, for razor vision."*

*We are quiet.*

*She shakes her head. "I don't know what that means."*

# Now Somebody Else Knows

■ ■ ■

I watched with razor vision. What I saw reminded me of the moment when the woman in the fur coat had slammed me into the coffee shop wall. And I knew why it had taken me so long to see what was happening, to witness the slow death—again—of a place I loved. We modern Americans are good at denying the truth of our senses. We deny the signs of betrayal. We pretend the ache in our heart has always been there. We forget the ancient practice of the deathwatch. Bearing witness. Carrying grief.

Heartbreak became business as usual. Not just mine, but the old-timers, the ranchers, the Hopi and Navajo and Apache, even the tourists who flocked to the Southwest, as I had, searching for what might be left of wild America.

In late May I drove down Oak Creek Canyon to teach Elderhostel. It was near sunset. The winding road was held by rock glowing like huge hands cupped over a candle. Spring trailed green over the canyon walls. I made myself see all of this. I didn't want to. I was myopic with fury, driving like the New Yorker I once was. If I didn't see the beauty of the natural web, maybe its annihilation wouldn't matter.

The Elderhostel couples were still eating when I walked into the beige-on-beige-with-neutered-Kokopelli dining room of the chain motel. The women and men were uniformly coupled and they seemed to be five to twenty years older than I was. When I went around the circle and asked them their names, the husbands, in most cases, spoke for their wives.

I read from my novel. The Elderhhostlers asked where to buy real Katsina dolls. I told them. They wanted to know if the Hopis make jewelry. I showed them my bear bracelet. They wanted to know where to buy one just like it, but maybe set with some turquoise. They wondered if pawn silver was still a good investment.

I read a few more pages and then stopped.

"I want to tell you something personal," I said. "A dear friend of mine is dying."

Their faces came alive. They were homies in that 'hood. I told them my friend was a meadow. They looked puzzled. Generously curious.

"I wonder," I said, "if any of you have lost a place you love, maybe a childhood place, or even now, as adults?"

People nodded.

"Could you tell us about it?" I asked.

There was silence.

"I saw some heads nod," I said. "How about putting your hands up if you have a memory of a place you lost?" There was no response, then four hands went up. Then a dozen.

Before I had a chance to choose someone, a man said, "Yes." He was bald, chubby, his sad face pink-cheeked. He looked, as do so many men of his generation, like an oddly withered twelve-year-old boy. He looked up into my eyes. "I left my childhood home and didn't go back for thirty-five years. When I did everything was changed. And I couldn't remember anything." He bowed his head.

"I'm so sorry," I said. He looked up. His eyes were wet. He looked around the room. "I'm glad I told you all," he said. "Now somebody else knows."

A woman patted his arm. The man behind him slowly raised his hand.


Ev came home for a week. He and I hiked out to Schoolhouse Draw, a wildflower meadow on national forest land just along our dirt road. We heard the place before we came around the curve and saw it. A couple dozen kids on fluorescent dirt bikes roared over the grass and flowers. They were video game apparitions gouging real dirt, ripping up spring grass and wildflowers.

"Razor vision," Ev said. The closest android slammed into high gear. "Razor hearing," Ev said. "We've got to do something." We decided to get them off the land—legally, so that the wildflower meadow would be protected not just for one summer, but for good.

I think back now to our decision and how it became a kind of medicine. Medicine for chronic pain, because though we won that battle, there were, there will always be, more. And more than medicine, our decision and our actions became deeper connections, linking us even closer, not just in our friendship but to the land itself.

Perhaps the greatest lesson the Western earth has taught me is this: only in being willing to have my heart break over the damage being done, and take heartbreak into action, have I felt truly connected with the places I love.

Perhaps it is as simple as this: I found myself walking along the rim of the Grand Canyon, remembering how we stopped the uranium mine, and I felt as though I was the canyon's daughter. Not merely *on* home ground, but part of it. And in accepting that knowledge, I keep my heart from becoming a cinder of rage.

*5/5/97: Spring snow, blessed be. I walk the dirt road, joyful that my face burns in the deep cold. I'm out of breath. I fall once and swear. Just past the house of a decent guy I once slept with absolutely without desire because I wanted somebody to want me, I hear a strange and familiar sound. A whirr. A not-quite-whooooosh. A raven flies across my path.*

*I remember my old home, the light more gray than this silver, my heart without Nicholas gray going charred. I walked to save my life. Into the Victorian cemetery that sprawled near the river. I forced myself to walk south, away from the path that led to Nicholas's shack.*

*I was lost in pain. Didn't notice twilight moving in, didn't care if the shadows around me held danger. Suddenly a huge flock of crows whooshed up from a skeletal November tree. My heart jolted. I realized I had laughed. The sound kept me alive for another night. Today my heartbeat is less precarious. All it will take is this one raven.*

*I pull my hood tighter. The snow comes faster and thicker. I'm grateful the storm has blocked out human sign, has muffled what highway noise there is, so that the raven's . . . I can't imagine how to write the sound of two wings carrying one black bird across my passage.*

*Whhhirrr . . . whissssss . . . not right. There is no human way to make the sound.*

I walked before dawn to what was left of the Meadow, finding my way in the quarter-light by cairns built by no human hand: a ring of limestone and wild geranium, an upended stump whose roots could have been markings on a map read purely by the senses. I walked at night, looked up to Orion, to a waxing moon, to the comet Hale-Bopp turning, turning, heading away. Tall Orion, broad-shouldered, narrow-waisted; the barely spilling moon, Hale-Bopp, even its name fat and goofy—their light shimmered in and out of the black web of pine. I stumbled out to see this. I stumbled back, tripping on rocks, catching my toe on a fallen branch. I caught my breath, let it go, as though I were singing, kin to those exiled Tibetan monks.

It seemed oddly right to find comfort there in the heart of impending loss. "I will come to you," I said, "until the gate and fences are up. And then I will visit from the other side."

Too often I wanted to leave Flagstaff, head out toward some little Western town that had yet to be discovered, but I was beginning to understand that absolute loss makes us offers we can't refuse. For sorrow. For love. For joy. For taking root. That is the nature of deep connection—it hooks us even as we try to run from it.

There were hours, even a day or two, of reprieve during Ev's brief return, if we drove far enough, walked far enough, left the highway long enough. On those trips, we would seem to be blessed with a sweet amnesia, as though only the present lay before us.

*5/21/97: I come awake on the lip of a little red-rock canyon I won't name for its own sake. I come awake for the first time in months with the words "Thank you." I open my eyes. The eastern sky is thin jade-blue. In front of me, a purple five-petaled blossom, no bigger than the pupil of a human eye, glows against a prickly pear.*

*The sun is just behind a far hill. The dark persimmon walls of the draw are still no-color. My butt aches, my hip seems ground against a boulder that has moved slowly up into my bones through the long, restless night.*

*I shift. My lower spine was damaged long ago. I have learned that spinal fluid pools around the vertebrae at night. I lie still, see my spine as dry and purely mineral as the bones you find in the country in which we are sleeping. If those desert skeletons were to rise up, they would move as I do, slow, slow—slow as the light beginning to pour up from behind the violet hills.*

*I hear Everett's voice. It is mournful. "There's still no half 'n' half."*

*We drink black coffee. "I'm pretending," he says, "that I'm in a foreign country where black coffee is a delicacy. I'm sitting here, in this non-American place, and I'm tasting this black coffee and saying to myself, 'Why, this is ever so much better than coffee with half 'n' half.'"*

*"And I," I said, "am sitting here not eating the bread and cheese I forgot to bring and thinking what a holy and cleansing experience this is."*

*Later he leads me to a break in the cliff face. We climb down. Seven A.M. sun falls on the spidery figures pecked into the black desert varnish. We say nothing. From our silence, from this place, from whatever moved that hand so long ago—our stories emerge.*

A few weeks after he left for Wyoming for the summer, I wrote him:

Bro. I know I can never do enough. And what I can do may be this: find the places where late-afternoon light burns copper, where an old stump and a young pine are side by side on a little hill. I can follow a dry watercourse uphill to a limestone overhang whose underside is luminous green moss. I can lie on my back under the damp rock and breathe mossy mineral air.

I can follow this pen, let it lead me into despair, and out. I can follow the pen to words that emerge in the greater world, maybe touch somebody, maybe get somebody off their ass.

I can paint the mask of my face black, and hang it next to the silk hanging of a God who is infinitely older than I am, and even hungrier. I can look out my window to your cabin and see shadows black as the old God's maw, and spring sun dazzling off the old tarp that covers the nearly used-up woodpile.

I can think of our friendship and feel hope.

# What Comes Around Goes Around

■ ■ ■

I wrote steadily, entered literary contests, sent essays and short stories to good magazines, kept my submissions moving out, knowing acceptance and rejection alike meant I was serving my apprenticeship. And then my cherished old laptop died. Without warning.

I spent two days in panic, two more debating whether to buy a typewriter, to slow down the record of what was moving too fast. I remembered how much I love to revise, gave in and bought a new computer. The saleswoman told me it had an internal modem. I felt as though I were buying drugs. Unpredictable drugs.

It took me a few days to open the box. And when I did, I found the software to put me online. I'd heard about the Web. I'd loved the idea of a network of words, an Indira's Web of creation, but the speed of its transmission seemed to be in anything but Animal Time.

Still, Ev was far away. And two of my kids were still in Asia. And my writing and side work barely paid the bills, especially a huge phone bill, so I decided to take a chance.

*6/12/1997: I set up the new computer today. I'm thoroughly intimidated by it. I turned it on, turned it off, and wrote a letter by hand. I'll tuck it into one of Nicole's cards, the one in which the woman turns into a tree made of ravens.*

*I'll drive to town and hand the letter to Patty to mail. She'll ask me how my writing is going. Altogether, I will live a few hours of my life as I do this. Who knows what I might see? A young orange flicker? An old guy riding a fat-tire bike with a happy dog sitting in the milk crate duct-taped to the front? A driver who actually uses the turn signal?*

*I can go on the Internet with this new computer. A connecting cord, a click, and I can go anywhere, except to a wildflower field unscarred by dirt bikes, the San Francisco Peaks before the pumice mine, the past in which I have read the notice of the development of the Meadow and have organized to stop it.*

*Still, what comes around goes around. I'm ready to take a spin.*

# DRASTIC MEASURES

# What Catches You When
# You Stop Running

■ ■ ■

Our Crazy Mountain Suite in Big Timber's Grand Hotel
was the nicest room in the hotel (with its own bath and
telephone), but we still found it impossible to connect a
notebook computer to the Internet, thus going cold
turkey off e-mail. By Stern standards, this was roughing it!

—JANE AND MICHAEL STERN,
*Roadfood*

What came next, a stalled trajectory of on-again, off-again e-mail
and computer game obsession, seems to me now as perfectly
shaped as southern Utah's Delicate Arch. The arch is sandstone
the color of flesh or coral or pomegranate, depending on light
and weather. It is an elegant skewed curve perhaps three hundred feet high. Through its heart, you see the indigo promise of
the La Sal Mountains. From the top of its keystone arc, you can
descend north or south, forward or back—if you are a very small
lizard.

I have been caught going forward, going back, making
progress as slowly as a tiny lizard on a huge stone arch. I disconnected into the flat blue of the Web, got lost in the icy computer

Scrabble tactics of the artificial opponent Maven (who more resembled my worst lover than anybody human). And then, choice by choice, I disconnected from the disconnections. To face just how ferocious living connected is, panic and re-sign on, find the drug not working and quit, which I have done and continue to do most imperfectly.

At first, e-mail seemed a great blessing. We, the local activist community which had come alive in late '97, used it to close Schoolhouse Draw to those motorized androids; to stop a developer from putting a golf 'n' gated second-home "community" next to a landlocked volcano crater wetland; to close a seven-story-deep pumice mine on our sacred mountains; to organize a handful of powerful (and endearingly Monty Pythonesque) community activist groups.

I loved being able to connect easily with editors, make changes in a twentieth of the time it once would have taken. I began to do radio commentaries with an NPR mentor, Cindy Carpien. She had moved to Flagstaff with her family to slow down, to give her kids a deeper, gentler place to grow up. Our brains met, knew each other and danced (most of the time) like Rogers and Astaire. E-mail was perfect to send our work to Washington, and to ease the chaos of long-distance team creating.

I sent essays to *Brevity,* an e-magazine, polished and essential as river pebbles, loved not waiting six months, a year, forever, to hear from the editor. My affection for e-mail grew when the time-challenged and saintly editor for the *High Country News* syndicated column service Writers on the Range signed me on. I didn't notice that I was beginning to go faster and faster, to return to the manic pace I had kept back east.

I used e-mail for far less noble reasons, and it used me. For a couple hundred faux connections with people who disappeared the night I pulled the modem plug. For bloodless intrigues with strangers, the most numbing an exchange with a brilliant poet who seemed unable to write anything but the most hackneyed erotica. I used it to blur the fear I felt coming home from a night at the casino, minus three hundred dollars I did not really have. And clicking to Inbox to keep the buzz going.

I used the Internet to sign up for credit cards, perhaps the worst decision of all.

When the chirpy "You've Got Mail" was silent, I slid computer Scrabble in the machine. Maven distracted me from the loss of my best ever Scrabble opponent, Ev. Maven was there during Ev's increasingly frequent absences, even on the autumn day in 1998 when Ev told me he was moving to Wyoming, maybe permanently, to run sled dogs and be full-time with a woman he loved.

Ev cried. I watched his tears dry-eyed and counted the minutes till I could turn on my computer and play Scrabble with the one opponent who wouldn't leave.

Now when I read my journals of those times, I see that even at the beginning, I knew I was moving over dangerous ground.

*May 1998: Yesterday I e-mailed a book review to the editor at Flag Live!, e-mailed my kids, and tried to get on the Web. By the time I went to bed, I felt like an android. Every thought and image in my mind seemed to be an icon, and I clicked and moved things and felt my thoughts shift constantly to how I could get on to the Web. I glanced down at a cat walking across the rug and found myself moving the computer mouse as though I could move the cat.*

*I remember that yesterday I did live in three dimensions, found a raven feather, fixed up the now six-trunked tree altar, fed the ravens, watched an inchworm travel the length of a pine branch for half an hour. I thought about how quickly and easily Human World can fog you and that I had better be prepared.*

*Especially since I love that fog.*

*A few weeks later: Today is the fiftieth anniversary of Roswell. When I go online, they are showing mesas we are told are Martian, two-dimensional as a small-town-theater stage set—all of this seen and transmitted by* Sojourner. *We are told we would be fascinated by all of this. Moving from here to there, from there to here. Mystery.*

*Now Mars is a cartoon. As is* Sojourner. *We humans name the Martian rocks: Barnacle Bill, Scooby Doo. There is no silence. There are no secrets. Nothing's sacred.*

*September 1999: I'm afraid of my inability to stay off e-mail, to stay away from Maven* [my computer Scrabble opponent], *of my inability to enter into my new novel. Every time I do, I think it is stronger, and then I remember something I wrote in early '97, about a tripped-out boy in front of McGaugh's downtown bookstore, a boy who is becoming molten silver, a boy slipping into the rain.*

*And I don't know what happened to my writing that way, writing as though I was going into white water.*

*There is something about the too easy ease of e-mail. The speed. Something the opposite of a river.*

In late autumn of that year I pulled a few old journals from the bookshelf and began to read. I found a wild river of words there. Sentences that went root-deep, dialogue bouncing off a midnight city street. When I read the writing in the more recent notebooks, I saw it was time for Code Blue, for the paddles to the chest, adrenaline straight into the heart. My real life was at stake.

It takes forever to hurt enough to begin to act, to take what feel like drastic measures. I'm sure I'm not alone in buying books that tell me how to change my life and leaving them half-read on the bedside table, because I'm exhausted from working seven to seven to get by. Or being hypnotized into hopeful voyeurism by movies in which a guy pays it forward or another guy builds it and people arrive. Most of us are filled with longing. For something. For something that we will begin tomorrow.

Or next week.

I was lucky to take the next steps back toward Animal Time. Not so much drastically as patiently, sometimes telling myself an unfinished story to make it through. *I can quit. For today.* I moved at a ragged pace that now seems elegant. A wayfinding. Deep into the present.

Each time I didn't check e-mail or the answering machine or race to the mailbox to see if anyone loved me, but opened my unfinished stories and read slowly till I came to the place where the words ran out, I felt hollow. It was not a welcome emptiness, but something disturbing.

For years the blank page had always brought excitement. My writing, which seemed to be the emptying of a bottomless pool of witness and recollection, had always left me filled. I wanted to jump into this new and unwelcome emptiness, write transitions I hadn't lived, race to endings I had no way of knowing. I wanted to earn my keep. Without the constant reassurance of messages, I didn't believe I deserved to be here.

Instead I began, slowly, slowly, to slow my pace. I drove at the speed limit, which not only lowered my blood pressure but infuriated the jet jockeys racing around me, made myself swallow what was in my mouth before I brought the fork back to my lips, stopped my mind's Indy 500 as I listened to a friend. I waited in line at Macy's Café without balancing my checkbook or taking notes for a future story.

I watched women with kids, or with helpless old parents, and

knew I was blessed to be conducting this experiment in slow mo
without being responsible for anyone else.

With the luxury of enough time to be faithful to being a
slow river. Getting ready to be a glacier. I found myself writing
more and more with a pen, letting there be blank paper
between    words    as    though    I    was    making    room    for
    what


            came


                next.

# What the Simplicity Gurus
# Leave Out

■ ■ ■

Mr. Fear stepped through the door of my cabin without knocking. Mr. Fear, my most faithful mainline squeeze. I remembered the days of *I'm scared, I'll do it,* and how I thought I'd left him behind. I knew about going through fear. I'd heard all the slogans: *Fear is False Evidence Appearing Real. Fuck the Fear—just do it. Fear is the opposite of Faith.* I'd read most of the earnest books about changing. Self-help. Buddhist. New Age. *Fear is an artifact of the past. Fear is an Illusion. Fear is the opposite of Love.*

Nobody, not the most earnest simplicity guru, not the most Westernized lama, not the most faux-elegant blond former business consultant turned motivational speaker has Mr. Fear's number.

Mr. Fear was, he *is,* shape-shifter par excellence, a skittering chameleon looking for all the world like my plan for success. Or murmuring in my ear, telling me I'd better check out this new, elusive guy, because, well, uh, you are getting older, honey. Mr. Fear is Loki grinning out of the new slot machine with silver moons and prancing unicorns. Pagan luck. Got my number.

He's the ghost in the white laboratory coat who tells me my cramps are cancer, the lapse in my memory the beginning of the end. He's the expert who can't believe an emotional chick like me would dare have an educated opinion.

Mr. Fear never, ever goes slow. And if you do, he's there to greet you. He grins. "Better hurry up," he says, "or you won't get yours."

But maybe you will. Maybe "yours" won't be what you thought you wanted. Maybe it will be what you need.

The more I slowed down, the more I knew how tired I was, how much I had forgotten how to slow-dance with the real moon. I had trouble falling asleep, finally lay awake one night in the deep quiet, thinking of how I would live if I had six months left. First I would disconnect from e-mail, then clean the cabin, throw away research not pertinent to fiction, return books I was not reading. I'd be in touch with those I love. I would camp, walk, write.

I thought of the day before, when I'd been babbling frantically to Cindy, my NPR producer, about what might happen, what might not happen, about something I hadn't done that I certainly would do, unless maybe I should do something else. Cindy, the ninety-mile-an-hour Beltway escapee, reached out and held me. "Hey," she said, "I thought you were going to slow down."

I listened to her. And to myself. I became a snail, coiling into my slowness. E-mail began to seem ghostly, the address book a graveyard. I wrote the two hundred fifty people on my list, told them I might be going offline, asked them to send me real mail addresses and phone numbers.

As I moved away from the hectic shimmer of the Internet, the slow light of the season carried me. The days shrunk, nights grew longer. The earth spun toward solstice.

Ev paid a brief visit from Wyoming, his new home. On a mid-December evening, he and I drove to Payson to gamble. We talked all the way, two scared, aging kids who'd been best friends for four years, who never ran out of passionate yakking and listening. We interrupted each other, spun with each other's fraying story line. Our laughter lasted much longer than a cyberclick.

Predictably, we lost our investments at the little casino, and drove back on the two-lane highway through a dark forest. A little fire glowed in the trees. Then another. Sparks leaped up and disappeared.

"Controlled burn," Ev said. "I love those words." We watched the glow of burning slash. Talked more. About obsession. About passion. Our words burned down to ash. Essential, as essential as the two meteors that arced above us, the first one slow, heading north, fat and foxfire green. The second one seemed to hang in the west. Below it, a young tree burned. Sparks billowed away from the crown. Pure incandescence. A slender torch, a pine Kali, fire ringing the base, sparks sailing off on the wind, the sky shining black, stars frozen, Orion huge and paralyzed, named and moved by our imaginations, his body no more than the shape of a story we tell ourselves.

I felt the wall around my heart crack, let in the vast, let in the tiny adventure of leaving the warm truck, stumbling over rocky earth, going toward the burning tree, under shining midnight, my breath and my friend's breath comets lit by fire.

We stopped. I breathed in smoke, coughed, held my palm near the burning bark, and felt my body come fully alive. Ev put his arm around my shoulders. I held his wrist, felt my friend's blood pulse under his skin. All in three dimensions, all in five senses, all in the sixth sense of the heart.

Solstice arrived. I woke December 22 welcoming the dawn, wrapped myself in my sleeping bag and sat on the back porch, watching the first shadows stretch over the frosted grass. One raven flew in. I waited for full light. I understood that despite the warnings of a dreadful new millennium, anything that slowed down my species, i.e., me, could bring only good, might even bring the gift of what we so frantically seek.

And then four days later, in the most unlikely of sanctuaries, in a paradox of canyon petroglyphs and neon, I was taken farther:

*12/25/99 (Paddlewheel Coffee Shop in the Colorado Belle Casino): I am going offline. I spent hours in Portal Canyon yesterday, sat in silence, doing nothing, watching the light cool. This morning, eating the second-best strawberry waffle I've had in a few weeks, seeing the two-story cowboy down at the Pioneer Casino wave his big arm up and down, smelling cigarette smoke and ozone from the slots, sucking in the pure oxygen the casino pumps in to keep us going, I can't imagine how I could have found e-mail interesting, or the Internet anything but a shadow.*

Two weeks after I had asked my Internet pals for real addresses and phone numbers, only a dozen people had responded: my four grown kids, my best Rochester friend, my best San Francisco friend. . . . All of the other respondents were people with whom I had been close long before I logged on. My buddies of the slow hand.

Perhaps my favorite response came from my youngest son, Matt, in Los Angeles. I found the envelope in my mailbox, covered with drawings of a Matt-morphed Bill the Cat:

Hi, Mom,

    This is a real letter. You can't save it to hard disk (unless you have a scanner). It's funny how we see advertising for Internet stuff that leads you to more advertising. The people I know who originally got into the Internet were rebels who wanted their own secret world away from advertising and censorship. It's funny how it has turned out.

    It disturbs me the most to see ads on TV for the

Internet. How absurd. I was watching the show *Antique Road Show* and realized that it too puts a price on our treasures. Years ago when I'd get tight for money, I would sell musical instruments and other treasures, but now I value what I have and realize it's important to keep these things. Money will always come and go, don't eBay (?) yourself.

I'm ten times more joyed to receive a letter than I am when e-mail appears. Maybe you'll get this before I arrive. But this is my response to your quitting e-mail.

Love, Matt

He signed off with a drawing of a rabbit ballerina.

I waited to see who else would write. And waited. I began to understand that an invitation to slow down might be, for most of us, an invitation to face what really matters. To pay attention to what we give attention. And facing that, to keep running at cyberspeed, letting what takes too much effort fall away. I was scarcely immune.

*12/29/1999: Ev tells me he is leaving Flagstaff for good, giving up the cabin. My stomach hurts. Shit. I hope it's not cancer.*

It is astonishing to me now to see that I had so lost touch with how I felt that I didn't connect a constant bellyache with my best friend leaving. Now when Ev leaves, I miss him; and when he returns, I welcome him with my whole heart. It has taken eight years to come fully into this friendship that lives in both fair weather and foul. It has been a long, clumsy dance. I'm grateful we have been carried by something that moves much slower than I.

And I'm grateful to have been free to approach going offline slowly, allowing myself to feel it fade from my world, allowed myself to feel, click by click, how unfeeling each so-called connection was. That freedom does not exist for those who earn their living online.

I went offline at 10:35 P.M., December 31. As I slowly pulled the modem cord from the jack and held it in my hands, I felt the same launch into icy beauty I felt when I finally cut my ties with Nicholas. As though I drifted somewhere beyond our galaxy, a tiny soul alone in a void black and bright as obsidian.

# Never Leave Your Machine

■ ■ ■

I began to relearn the lesson I learned when I quit drinking, when I longed for a lover who did not long for me, when I tackled the endless job of saying no: *An addict doesn't stop once.* An addict doesn't hit the jackpot of freedom. Life without using is day after day of stopping and stopping and stopping again. Robert Downey Jr. has said it best: *I've got a loaded gun in my mouth and I love the taste of the metal.*

There'd better be company along the way. Elders. Users. Kin whose blood runs with the same longing for whatever gets you high. Kin who understand that the most dangerous words in the English language are "So what?"

*1/15/2000: I have the impulse to log on every time I have a pause in my day, feel anxious, feel empty. I don't. I can't. Though I could reconnect in a big-city heartbeat.*

*Yesterday my phone rang three times, two real people and a wrong number. There were two bills in the mailbox. I went to a meeting, called Roxane, and stood with Robin in front of Home Depot with a picket sign that read SHOP LOCAL.*

*This morning I thought of my friend Max talking about staying out of casinos, saying, "All I wanted to do was sleep." Me too. I'm terrified of the Big Sleep and all I want to do is sleep. E-mail was like playing a daily slot. You slide your time in the slot, click,*

*and who knows what jackpot might appear—a letter from an old*
*lover, a seduction from a new one, acceptance of a story, a new*
*enviro-crisis into which you can disappear. Or there's nothing but*
*forwards and bad jokes—and you watch the credits drop to zero.*

I stopped. I stayed stopped. I would look for the beckoning
Internet server icon on my screen and see the pure blue space it
had once occupied. My gut would tighten. I would put the computer to sleep, pull on my hiking boots, and head up the snowy
dirt road. Or wash dishes. Or pace my little living room, picking
up papers and moving them to the next cluttered tabletop.

Now and then, and now and then more frequently, I would
do nothing. And find myself, in a minute or twenty, clicking
open an essay or a story and going to work. My fingers on the
computer keys or wrapped around a pen followed paths that
had not yet been made. Spirit lines, leading me away and leading me back.

Words spilled from the pool of witness and recollection. And
as they emptied out, I felt full. For a while. And then somehow,
almost mindlessly, I would drive south to the little Apache
casino, not guessing I was doing what is so easy to do when we
leave something necrotic and beloved behind.

*1/16/2000: Report from the tedious—I managed to walk out of*
*the casino last night with twenty bucks of the hundred I took in.*
*Had I left an hour earlier, I could have walked out up five bucks.*
*All of this, the winning, the losing, due to the compelling charm*
*of the new Penguin slot machine.*

*There is nothing quite like seeing the beautiful sunset-lit ice-*
*berg show up on the left side of the screen, and a gold coin show*
*up on the right. There is a pause. And then, a perky little pen-*
*guin appears. He moves through all fifteen positions on the nine-*
*line game. He is wild. So any potential combination you have*

*becomes a hit. He completes the hit, starts to slide on the video ice, and falls on his little penguin butt. The credits mount. He goes to the next position and you, the lucky slot player, perhaps sip on your free watery beverage and grin.*

*I left the casino at twelve-thirty* A.M. *and drove up the hill without incident, except for a tiny shooting star. Someday I will read this and go, "What the fuck was I doing?" or read this and want to jump in my truck and head straight for the little Penguin vampire!*

Friends have been baffled by my devotion to casinos. They point out that gambling addiction in huge ugly buildings that suck air-conditioning, electricity, water, and human lives does not quite jibe with being Ms. Greenjeans or an ecstatic. They haven't a clue.

It is not Ms. Greenjeans that loves casinos, nor the ecstatic, nor even the old woman I am becoming. From the instant I push through the smoked-glass doors into rainbow neon and bells to the infinite abundance of the delicious lousy buffets; to the possibility that the Queen of the Nile machine on the end of the row, the perfect machine in the perfect location, holds the outrageous gift I didn't even dare ask for to the moment I have to leave, I am an eight-year-old girl on Christmas morning.

As long as the money holds out, as long as the ATM is my friend, I return to the endless exquisite moment when my brother and I stood in the dark hall at the threshold of Christmas, and the rush when the rainbow lights leaped up and we were transported into the jingle of my mother's candle chimes, a wealth of mysterious packages, and the guarantee of surprise.

In the casinos I am freed from my aging body, from the inexorable speed with which the rest of my life seems to be moving. I'm not alone. Research links the chemistry of gambling addiction to the chemistry of cocaine. I remember an aging friend, a guy terrified of getting old, telling me that cocaine was like being fourteen again. Who needs coke, who needs estrogen when a perfectly legal drug that won't give you a heart attack or blood clots lies forty-five minutes away?

I think now of how gambling carries me, and how when I am online, e-mail can take over in those rare times when gambling fails. The failure is not about losing, nor about money, though my last five years in the casinos cost me at least thirty thousand dollars, thirty large I did not have, thirty large I borrowed, at 17 percent interest, maybe more.

I, like many other women, did not play to win. I played for Christmas morning. I played because in the casinos *nobody* was the boss of me. As my gambling sisters know, in front of the slot screen, my time was my own.

Sometimes the magic didn't work and I found myself trapped in what seemed like a bad acid trip, ground glass moving in my veins, the parking lot outside the casino 130 degrees of hell, my truck not air-conditioned, and one more free night on my hotel comps. So I would stay. Hit the money machine next morning, grab a double bad coffee to go, and hunker down at my favorite machine. By the time I left, my brain and spirit were sandpapered, and I'd be nattering to myself, "Next time will be different."

And a week later, I'd say, "So what." Besides, there were the people. The stories. The moments when Ev and I would look at each other without a word, knowing we were taking field notes in our brains, for another war story, another reason to go on the gambling highway.

"Remember," he'll say. "Remember Pipe Springs." The little Paiute casino is no longer there. It was no bigger than a double-wide trailer. The chubby cocktail waiter with the silver feather in his ear would stop at your side, say, "Like a nice cold beverage?" and hold out a tray of plastic glasses filled with generic cola. And

there was the night Ev and I were on our way to the Big Rock
Candy Mountain up near I-70 and stopped for a break. We
played a couple hours, then I had to take a leak. I ran my credits down to zero and headed for the ladies' room. When I came
back, a scrawny cowboy had shoved a dollar in *my* machine and
on his first spin hit one hundred and twenty-five bucks. The
change girl smiled at me. "Oh," she said gently, "that's too bad.
But you should *never* leave your machine."

Now it seems ironic that the one place I could and do forget
about what's happening to the West is the perfect microcosm of
what's happening to the West, a place with few windows, constant noise, fake air, where the theme all day and night is "More
is better." The paradox does not escape me. I quit gambling
once, twice, felt bored and weary, felt bereaved, and went back.

Then in late February 2002, a suspiciously speedy guy in a suspiciously anonymous white rental car rebounded off a big
Dakota into the left front fender of my little pickup. Despite
growing exposure as a writer and countless bailouts from friends,
dumb luck, and the Big Loan Officer in the Sky, I found myself
with a possibly fatally wounded twelve-year-old truck, rental car
bills, and matching bank and credit card balances—$0.

"Maybe," said Ev, who had come back for the winter, "it's
time for something drastic."

"Like what?" I said.

"Like quitting gambling."

"Maybe," I said, "you need to go back to Wyoming."

"Maybe," he laughed, "you need to face reality."

Nine days later I took myself through a ritual. That was the
easy part.

*2/15/2002: I set my orange La Santisima Muerte candle in
the heart of my Western altar. I believe West is the direction of the
Goddess Who Eats That Which Is No Longer Useful. She is the*

*Goddess of Death, Our Lady of That Which Goes Around and Comes Around.*

*The candle is surrounded by chunks of obsidian, photographs of beloved animals and people: Bad Kitty, Nessathedog, Dead Bill, the ex. A plaster Mexican goddess sits in the window behind the altar. Her face is twisted in agony. She could be dying, she could be giving birth. Dead Bill the ex thought she was sexy. Bad luck. She claimed him.*

*I light the candle. It is morning, the flame not much more than a shimmer against the soft light. My intention is steady as a forge.*

*I placed my last slot bet nine days ago. I loved every millisecond of it. Win or lose. My pal, Everett, looked over at me from his machine. "Ready to go?" he said.*

*"Never," I said. "Yes."*

*We drove out into the desert, to a cow-fouled spot near a big juniper. We drank coffee, played Scrabble. We watched light move molten over the cholla, red-gold slow as a good lover's hands, and I thought of the neon of the casino. How it jitters. How I love it so much.*

*We knew we were quitting. I can't speak for him, but I have burned through thirty thousand dollars in five years—and more. Because I am a binge player, the neuronal currents of my brain, fragile at best, have surged and ebbed the way a flash flood slams down a desert wash. What's left behind is scraped and twisted.*

*Cocaine is baby food next to gambling.*

*So this morning I lit La Santisima Muerte and cut up my slot club cards, the bright souvenirs of the best love affair in which I've ever been seduced, neglected, reseduced, and left flat. The double handful of slot cards have hung for three years on the kitchen wall on bungee cords, purple, yellow, blue, and red. The lucky player gets to pick. The cards tell you that you are Royalty, Preferred, heir to Mountains of Money. When you slide them into a machine, the points add up. You can claim free rooms, meals, gifts, and mugs: a room you pay six hundred dollars for, slid twenty by twenty into the nickel machine; a three-hundred-dollar plate of beef ribs; a five-hundred-dollar kaleidoscope; a mug that for what it cost might have been made of sterling silver.*

*And, quite literally, the casino has your number.*

*I look at the wavering flame of the Death candle and pick up the first slot card. Colorado. Six hours on Queen of the Nile, sitting next to two gay men who shrieked "Queens Rule" every time we hit a bonus. I cut the card in four pieces, sever the yellow bungee cord as I once cut imaginary ties to a man I loved dearly.*

*Nevada. Along a dying river. Cleopatra. Fifteen thousand credits piling up so fast I can barely feel I'm winning. Belgian waffles with strawberries and whipped cream. The card is yellow, the cord gray. I cut. I slice through magic.*

*Arizona. Giving to the Apaches. If you are lucky, you get an iceberg glowing on the right side of the screen, a gold coin on the left. An adorable penguin appears and moves through all the positions on the grid. He is wild. After he completes a win, he slips and falls on his penguin butt. I'll miss him forever.*

*There are a dozen cards. I watch them pile up in the trash basket. Sorrow fills my heart. The loss is incalculable. How my mouth goes dry with excitement on the drive west. That first hit of cold smoky air on my face, the smell of ozone, of possibility. The stories: There was the heavyset young mother in sweatpants, sneakers, and an old jacket, who sat at three A.M. on the the fourteenth step of the red-carpeted Grand Staircase leading down to the casino floor, reading a Bible to her stocky Chicano eleven-year-old son. . . .*

*. . . and a scrawny blonde in a beautifully cut pinch-waist brown tweed jacket with frayed velvet collar and cuffs, brown double-knit bell-bottoms, delicate miniheel pumps, a huge faded gold Xmas corsage. Most of her teeth were brown stumps. She*

*handed the cashier two dollars and walked off, grinning, with her roll of nickles. . . .*

*. . . and the drunk old babe who showed me the gold-and-diamond watch her hubby gave her, and told me she was from Scottsdale. "It's different there," she said, "real classy.". . .*

*. . . and Betty, the sixty-two-year-old change "girl" who told me that after a while, you don't hear the squawks and feedback coming from the pager clipped to her shirt. . . .*

*. . . and her friend, Monica, a butch gal with a waxed crew cut, who tells me to wait while she gets her friend who has drawn the most beautiful Nativity scene in crayons and turned it into cards. . . .*

*. . . and a chubby girl whacked out on speed letting a man buy her breakfast. He watches her pick at her food. His lips are wet.*

*The bungee cords lie tangled in the trash. I tie the plastic bag shut. I will carry it to the Dumpster. I will drop it in and close the lid.*

*What happens next is not mine to say. The Goddess of the West runs that show. She Who Eats That Which Is No Longer Useful, Our Lady of the Next Blessed Breath. I am at her mercy. For all I know, her favorite words are: "Never Leave Your Machine."*

The aftermath was predictable. Gray, gray time. Acid rain poured through my bloodstream. My gut ached. My eyes hurt. I was sure I had a dozen fatal diseases.

I lived through Hanta virus, flesh-eating strep, and the plague, only to have Mr. Fear grab me by the scruff of the neck. "Hey," he said. "It's me. We're going to take a little trip." We went back into all the cracks in my life I had tried to fill. Into terrors I thought I had left behind. I had no choice. I was horrified to find myself in those old, old places again, knowing I had moved steadily toward them with every bet I placed. And furious this last glittering refuge had failed me.

I spent weeks thinking I couldn't think. I am astonished at the power of that withdrawal. It was as though a huge hand shook me steadily, and a voice deep within repeated again and again, "This is what it's like to run on empty, sweetheart. Next time it might be worse."

# MEDICINE

The power the bad ones use and the power the healers use comes from the same place. The difference is the bad ones are greedy for it and the healers are shy of it. They know power is to be used only for medicine. It is a burden.

—*Violet*

*Flagstaff, 1989*

# Doing Nothing

■ ■ ■

A scrap of paper lies on the rug. I am rushing to get bookstore information to my Nevada editor by FedEx, a book of cartoons to my son in Los Angeles, a book review to a friend in Wyoming. I am all over the map.

I pick up the paper. Better to clean than write.

Here is what I read:

> *Be a blank*
> *sheet of paper.*
> *Be a spot of ground*
> *where nothing is growing,*
> *where a seed*
> *could be planted,*
> *perhaps from*
> *the absolute.*
>
> —RUMI

I follow Rumi's instructions, pull the old rocker up to the woodstove. I make my mind blank. Feel afraid. Wait out the fear, and find myself remembering one of the few gifts television gave me.

By the time I got involved with Dead Bill for our fourth and final go-round, I hadn't watched television for decades.

Rocky and Bullwinkle were my last clear memories of the tube.

Dead Bill drank beer. Dead Bill loved his recliner. *Ergo,* Dead Bill loved TV. Usually I read while he surfed through news, sports, and soft porn, but one night by pure luck, he clicked on *Northern Exposure.* It was Xmas and the town of Cecily was celebrating with ravens. Raven highball glasses, raven lights, and, at the end of the show, a Tlingit production of *Raven Steals the Sun.* On national television. I could not believe my eyes.

Dead Bill and I watched every episode till we broke up and my access to TV was gone, but what remains in my memory is a scene in which the young transplanted urban doctor asked his Tlingit assistant, Marilyn, how she could sit without doing anything.

She offered to teach him. He sat in the big chair behind his desk, his hands on the armrests, and smiled nervously. I can't remember her exact words, but they were simple, maybe, "Now, you just do nothing."

"No problem," he said. A millisecond later, the camera panned in on his fingers twitching.

Could have been me. When e-mail, Maven, and lining up three bonus pyramids at the casino didn't work, I became my younger frazzled self, the inventor of multitasking. I wrote NPR commentaries in my head while I walked the trail at Buffalo Park, cleaned up my computer desktop while I talked on the phone. I never left the cabin without something to carry to the truck, never entered the cabin without water or wood or the groceriesnewspaperspostersslaundry I had taken from the truck. I seemed to forget everything I had ever learned about slowing down in those first days of my immigration to the Southwest.

I forgot my grown son's words: "What really hurt when we were kids, Mom, wasn't your drinking. It was that you were never there. YOU WERE ALWAYS FUCKING WORKING." I forgot that to know a place, the seven-trunked tree a half mile down the road, the patch of globemallow shimmering near the old ruin, the perfect long southern line of the sacred mountains, to be intimate with those pure intersections, I had to visit them through seasons, through weather—through the seasons and weather of my own heart. I couldn't connect with them at a dead run.

In racing away from the losses I saw in the mirror, in my life, and most ferociously in the Western earth, I raced away from joy. And then I remembered my mother telling me when I was little that they had never had to punish me for bad grades. "If you came home with four As and a B, the only grade you told us was the B. And you promised us you would do better. We never had to say a word."

I remembered believing that if I could just get it right, *It,* the big It, the big everything, she would not get sick again. I remembered how work had blocked terror in my twenties and losses in my forties. In some ways, it is the perfect nonprescription drug. You can use it anywhere. You can take it anytime. PRN.

My profession is dangerous for the work junkie. Writing is hypothetically endless, especially if you waited decades to begin. There is a story about Tess Gallagher, the poet and widow of writer Ray Carver, how she was cleaning his desk and found the beginnings of a hundred stories. They haunt me. Carver's unfinished stories, unlike Scheherazade's, did not save *his* life.

So I write every day. *Weekend* has no meaning, because I inevitably pick up the Sunday papers intending to relax with them and find myself four pages into Section A, furious, scribbling notes and plotting the next essay, the one that will save, if not the world, at least the New Southwest.

I am a perfect failure at perfection.

Thanks be to Leonard Cohen for reminding us there are

cracks in everything. If the earth can bear my species' imper-
fections, then I can endure the cracks in my own hard path
toward grace. I might even manage to feel compassion. For
myself. For my human kin.

# Daily

■ ■ ■

*I write a little every day,*
*without hope,*
*without despair.*

—ISAK DINESEN, BY WAY OF
RAYMOND CARVER

*2/14/2000: Two coffeehouse habitués told me people were taking bets on how long I'd stay offline. I was truly amazed at their words. I have no inclination to go back. I told them the last year of e-mail felt like the middle of an upstate New York July noon, 98 degrees, 98 percent humidity—with mosquitoes.*

*I came home and bagged clothes for Goodwill, wish I could so easily bag friendship. I know Ev leaving is an invitation— to bare bones, loneliness, my pen moving like a snake over unmarked sand. I'm ready but I already miss him. I can feel the uneasiness that moves into my cells when I go solo.*

*Still writing in the company of my students last night, I remembered I have a mysterious life. Tomorrow I will be in the Mohave. I'll pack my stove, my bedding. I'll go alone, sleep under a sky as vast and fiery as the waters of the Johnstone Strait. Green fire. Phosphorescence. Stars long dead. Burning.*

*It's time again.*

Beware of vows. Beware of epiphanies. I am back online. It is easy to persist when what is gone are mosquitoes, hard to resist when the trouble gone was also beloved and keeps hanging out at the spirit's periphery like that bad boy with the James Dean cheekbones who you knew would use his switchblade charm on your heart.

Here is the mantra of the devout addict: *Maybe next time will be different.*

"Sit on your hands," say those old drunks smoking their cigarettes and drinking lousy coffee one day. Freedom lies in limitation, the Buddhists teach. In counting your breath again and again. Day after day. A story grows a word at a time. *I write a little every day . . .* every day.

Tell all of that to my friend who had snooped outside his beloved's trailer and heard her moaning in the arms of another guy. "It was twenty seconds at a time," he told me. Enough time to say the Serenity Prayer over and over again—with variations: Grant me the serenity to accept the things I cannot change; the courage to change the things I can; and the wisdom to know the difference.

Grant me the fucking serenity to fucking accept the fucking things I cannot fucking change. . . .

One full night from midnight to six A.M., a thousand hours, centuries, aeons, lying on his bed, staring up at the cabin ceiling, muttering out loud because that way he didn't hear the echoes of her moans in his mind. And the next night. And the next. Not picking up a drink. Not going back to her trailer. Not picking up the phone. Persisting.

Persisting for a week, a month, a year till the day he saw her on the street, and crossed to the other side. And called me, his voice shaking, saying, "I did it. This shit works. Use it if you ever need to."

I did. Not with a lover, but with the fiendish and ever accessible Maven. It took me three tries to permanently get rid of computer Scrabble. Ludicrous, right? But I was fully capable of sitting down after lunch thinking I would play a game or two and then get back to my novel. Twilight would burn blue in the big southern windows and I would realize that while I had finally beat Maven at the 1900 level, a hungry cat was whimpering around my ankles, I had to pee, and another precious day was gone. A day in a writer's life, a life in which the writer had spent thirty-three years engaged in damn near anything but writing.

It is stunning that those of us who can persist perfectly in our compulsions—against all common sense, against all awareness that what once felt miraculous now feels dead, against all intelligence and intention—find it thoroughly daunting to persist in letting go of that which eats us alive, and take hold of the small miracles we have ignored for so long.

All we have is breath. All we have is pulse. All we have is this instant. All gifts. Neither deserved nor undeserved. All worthy of our persistence. All worthy of the space that only we can make—for freedom, for connection. And most assuredly, for mistakes.

Sometimes, that's how it goes. We are creatures moved by the tides in our brains and spirits. For some of us, those tides are tsunamis. They overwhelm us. Monthly, weekly, daily. In ordinary time.

For me a week is sometimes more than I can bear. The best I can do in stopping anything is manage from dawn to dusk, from waking to sleeping. And, perhaps, the next day do the same. It is as though the spirit is muscular, and persistence an extreme sport that can never be mastered. There is only practice . . . and the echo of Scheherazade's voice. Telling a story. One story a night. Winning herself one more day to live.

# Occupying Less

■ ■ ■

Thank God for the things I do not own.

—TERESA DE AVILA

I can't fully explain why the less I have, the more connected I feel. The link between not owning and belonging is cellular. I remember the three days alone at Boyd's Pond, how I had packed enough for a family of six. And the first solo trip west, my bags filled with books and embroidery and patchwork I never touched. My first river trip, I carried a Walkman and a dozen tapes. They never left the dry bag.

I love buying clothes at Goodwill and returning them when they no longer feel right on my body. I buy books in our local bookstores, then recycle them at another. My cabin is crammed with art and feathers and rocks, but most of the furniture was here when I rented the cabin: two battered dressers, raw pine kitchen cupboards, and a dozen shelves made from milk crates and old lumber. The only items left from my life back east are my rolltop desk and the secondhand library chair Nicholas gave me for my thirty-ninth birthday.

My truck is twelve years old. It has four cylinders. There have been casino trips when I pushed it to eighty-five miles an hour.

There is just enough room under its camper shell for me to sleep. I have driven across country with a food box, stove, and a backpack full of clothes. None of this is because of political beliefs; all of it is because it brings me joy, a joy mysterious and ordinary.

It is strange to remember the years when mail-order catalogs filled the kitchen table, when an East Coast friend gave me a cloth bag carrying the logo WHEN THE GOING GETS TOUGH, THE TOUGH GO SHOPPING. Most of the forty-dollar T-shirts and museum reproductions and high-tech garden tools that I never used are gone, given as gifts or taken to Goodwill. Not one of them gave me even half the pleasure their absence has.

I got lucky. A wild bird brought me to this jackpot of less. A juvenile orange flicker came into my cabin one August night a dozen years ago. I tried to catch it. The bird fled behind the stove, beyond my reach. The cats gathered in the kitchen. I banged the side of the stove. The bird was silent. I had no choice but to let it be.

I went back to bed and tried to sleep. There was silence in the kitchen. One by one, the cats curled up around me. I watched the dark in the windows begin to fade and fell asleep.

When I woke the cats were gone. I climbed out of bed, lit my morning candle, and walked into the living room. The cats sat in a row at the foot of the old couch. The flicker sat on the back-rest and regarded the cats and me with perfect calm.

I opened the back door. Morning was delicate green, light and shadow playing across the pine duff. I pulled off my old work shirt and gathered the flicker into its folds. The bird did not move.

I carried the bird to the back porch and unfolded the shirt. For a long moment the bird rested in the cloth. I thought it might be tangled and took it into my hands. Again it was still.

Then with a wing-beat that could have been a breath, the bird flew out straight toward a young pine.

I will never forget the sensation of release. And the four orange-and-black feathers I found lying on the kitchen floor.

Enough. More than enough.

# The Essential

■ ■ ■

In the Ojibwe language the word [love] does not exist in the same sense—there is love out of pity, love out of kindness, love that is specific to situations or to the world of stones, which are alive and called our grandfathers.

—LOUISE ERDRICH, *The Last Report on the Miracles at Little No Horse*

Perhaps four years ago, I was invited to a Navajo ceremony. The invitation came on the morning of the evening it would occur from a man I barely knew. It arrived not by e-mail or letter, but by phone. He said the ceremony was for the mountains sacred to the Navajo, and for the health of the planet. The singer, the *hataalii*, was a highly respected man. I could invite a few friends. He gave me directions to the place where the ceremony would be held. He didn't wait for my answer.

I hung up the phone and went to the old blue rocker on my back deck. I looked out toward the twin pines. I had plans for the evening, a date with a distinctly probable possible. It had been a year since anyone had touched me. Hummingbirds strafed each other in and out of the trees. I waited for some ancient wisdom. Harold, the Forrest Gump cat, jumped in my lap. I scratched him behind the ears and decided my fifty-eight-year-old wisdom would have to do.

I went back in the house, picked up the phone, and canceled the date. I called a friend, then another, a woman and man who had been my companions in the work to save the caldera known as Dry Lake from development. The woman and I agreed to meet and drive together. Then I remembered the other information I'd been given. "It is not quite an all-night ceremony, but almost." If we did not want to camp, we would drive home on a killer highway long past midnight. We decided to each take our own truck.

"Should we bring food," she asked, "and an offering for the *hataalii*?"

I didn't know. After I hung up, I thought back to planning meetings with the Havasupai during our resistance to the uranium mine. I remembered how the details of each meeting seemed nothing but bumbled moments, how so often we Anglos laughed about Grandmother Time, then got mad, then laughed again because always, always, what emerged was stronger and deeper than anything any of us, Havasupai or Anglo, could have logically planned. And in the long run the mine had not been sunk.

Late in the afternoon I got the cats squared away with food and water, told my neighbor I'd be gone till sometime the next day, loaded my gear into my truck, and headed out. I stopped at the local market for five boxes of bright sugar cookies. I'd already tucked a chunk of obsidian into my pack. If the opportunity presented itself to give the rock to the *hataalii*, I would.

Indigo shadows drifted down from the cinder cones. I cruised to the bottom of the long hill out of East Flagstaff as though I were just another shadow. I had begun to feel the gentle hollowing I always feel before a ceremony.

I found the turn and bumped over a cattle guard onto a wide

dirt road. The directions were impeccable as long as I didn't think too hard. I turned onto what appeared to be nothing, dropped into a little wash that seemed impassable, emerged on the other side onto a two-track that led me west, then south.

Smoke rose a quarter mile ahead. I followed the gray plume, bumped off the two-track onto flatland a few hundred feet from a brush shelter, and parked next to a late-model King Cab pickup with a Vietnam campaign bumper sticker on the back. I opened the car door and was surrounded by the fine fat scent of mutton broiling.

I will keep the details of the ceremony private in respect to the Navajo except to say that near midnight I found myself breathing four prayers into a shimmering powder of ground minerals and corn pollen I held in my palm. Without question. With perfect trust.

We woke early next morning, drank strong black coffee, ate fry bread. The *hataalii* and his apprentices had gone on ahead. We climbed into our trucks and followed the big King Cab back out to the highway and onto the dirt road that takes you up into a meadow below the heart of the sacred mountains, the mountains the Dine call Do'okosl'iid.

We drove into the campground near the meadow and stopped. Morning sun slanted through the dark pines. The scent of the trees surrounded us. I wondered how I had been lucky enough to be brought to this light, in this shadow, breathing pure green. And then I stopped wondering and did what I was told.

One of the old Dine began to have trouble walking the trail to the next part of the ceremony. We were going uphill, probably at 8,500 feet. The man who had invited me to the ceremony and his friend linked hands. The old Dine sat on the human chair. They carried him up the trail.

I watched one of the apprentices approach a small gray boulder. He paused, and then, with a tenderness I have only seen in the hands of a mother or father, he touched the rock. I thought of the soul-sickness that had gripped me when I saw how the developers' bulldozers had altered the rocky contours of the Meadow, and as the Dine man's gnarled hands caressed the little boulder, I knew what I had felt was sanity.

The *hataalii* and his apprentices prepared to bury our prayers. As they sang, I heard a low roar. I looked around, saw nothing, looked up, thinking a plane or helicopter flew over. The sky was clear. At the finish of the ceremony, the *hataalii* asked us to tell him if we had heard anything. I couldn't bring myself to speak. I thought I would be judged.

The West has been flooded for the last decade or so with non-Indians who believe they can be Indians. These wanna-bes have appropriated Native American sacred symbols—Kokopelli, Mimbres animals, petroglyphs—and slapped them on everything from drink coasters to men's boxer shorts. I once listened to an Anglo woman read "Hopi wisdom" from a book written by another Anglo woman during a Crone workshop for which twenty Anglo seekers had paid a hundred bucks apiece—including me. No chance was I going to risk opening my mouth about the low roar I had heard.

Then as I walked down the trail on the living stone of the mountain between pine trees centuries older than my grandiose self, I realized I had no right to be silent. The *hataalii* led us to the parking area and gathered us in a circle. Again he asked us to tell him if we had seen or heard anything unusual. He said our words would help him and his apprentices to interpret what their next steps should be.

There was silence. I looked up at Do'okosl'iid. I saw how tiny I was. "I heard something," I said. The *hataalii* waited. "I heard a low roar. I thought it was a plane, but the sky was clear."

The *hataalii* looked at one of his apprentices, then back at me. "Did it sound like a bear?"

I wanted desperately to answer yes, but I knew that was not what I had heard.

"No," I said, "not a bear."

The *hataalii* asked me from what direction I had heard the sound. I told him. He asked the rest of the circle if they had heard the sound. One of the apprentices nodded.

I waited until the circle had dispersed and approached the *hataalii*. "There's more," I said.

He waited.

"The sound was the sound a rock would make if it could make sound."

The *hataalii* did not laugh. He did not look at me as if I were crazy. "Everything on the mountain," he said, "has spirit. Especially the rocks."

That is my first essential. Everything has spirit. We are bedrock. And I am less sturdy than sandstone, more permeable than basalt. When I forget this knowledge, I am lonely. When I deny it, I am lost.

# SPIRIT LINE

■ ■ ■ ■ ■ ■ ■ ■ ■ ■ ■ ■ ■ ■ ■ ■ ■ ■

If the weaver believes in the spirit life she does not cage color in with a border. Instead, she leaves a small opening through which the spirit can escape, thus assuring her future rugs will be beautiful and blessed by the spirits.

—Noel Bennett,
*The Weaver's Pathway*

# Road Time

■ ■ ■

Desire and loss move in all directions. In switchbacks. Toward dead ends. Back to awkward grace, forward into the unknown. They move on Road Time. When you're lucky, you travel with them. Scheherazade rides shotgun and you all swap stories.

In late summer 1998 I drove out to visit Ev in Wyoming and took a four-hundred-mile detour so I could play slots in a little Nevada gambling town. There in a cramped and smoky casino lounge I began to come home. Toward the things I have always loved most deeply, even when that love was no more than remembering. Music. The Hook. The Unknown. Telling stories. And though I didn't know it as I walked into neon and black mirrors, my connections with my grown children.

I settled down at my favorite slot. The announcer bounced onto the stage. "And now," he said, "Natalie and Daemine." I kept playing. Then a man's voice, sweet and smoky as good barbecue, filled the room. I turned away from my gambling to listen. I remembered after-hours joints in Rochester, and the summer evening my lover Michael and I had heard the blues drifting in the lakefront air over Buffalo, swung off the thruway and spent the rest of the night in the company of Buddy Guy, Howlin' Wolf, and a hundred drunk and stoned dancing fools. It saddened me that those times seemed a century ago, that I couldn't remember the last time a guitar riff or perfect phrasing had opened my heart.

After the last set, I asked Natalie how they could perform night after night to an audience of gamblers bungee-corded to their slot machines. "This is just what we do," she said. "We have to." I vowed to myself to write a commentary about them for NPR. I wanted a hundred thousand people to hear her words and Daemine's voice—and pay tribute to musicians who just do what they do.

I caught their act a few other times. In the hardscrabble stateline towns of Mesquite and Wendover. Each time their music pulled me away from my machine. Each time they cracked my heart. I carried their story for three years, cooked it, stirred it up, felt it coming together—rhythm and blues, and black-mirror walls, and gifted people who work hard because that's what they do.

In early 2000 I drove west to begin writing their story. Daemine was playing at the Kokopelli Lounge in the Edgewater Casino in Laughlin, Nevada, a gambling town built a few decades ago on the shore of the Colorado River, at the eastern edge of the Mojave Desert. Neon and joshua trees. Twist my arm.

Here are my notes from the Kokopelli Lounge:

. . . *old guy with a cane hobbles in, hanging on to tables to move himself along. Drum kit glitters under red lights. Two sleek gray hairs, the requisite cashmere cardigan slung over the guy's shoulders. "Respect," now an old oldie, on the sound system. The wife of the gray-haired couple snaps her fingers the Republican way. And a-one, and a-two.*

*Black velvet backdrop with glued-on glitter. Lights go blue. Lounge begins to fill. Guy next to me says, "All right, real musicians." The television over the bar glows surreal. Nobody pays attention. A gold-dusted Kokopelli sparkles on the wall. The back wall is red velvet, the slots jangling on the other side of the curtain.*

*The band burns through a warm-up, then the distinctly non-decaffeinated guitar player grabs the mike and whispers, "Here he is. The young man who has been doing this forever." Daemine strolls out in a bright red jacket and a patchwork vest. There is a long pause, a vampy intro, and Daemine closes his eyes. "Me . . . and . . . Mrs. Jones . . . we got a thing goin' on."*

*Natalie has come in. She stands against the back velvet curtain. Daemine waves the band into a slow vamp and asks for the spot to shine on her. "That's my beautiful wife," he says. He tells us how they met and sang together for thirteen years. I remember my first sight of her, red satin hot pants, long, long legs, her dark hair catching the silver spotlight. Now she grins. Daemine steps back into the spot. When I turn to look, she is rocking back and forth in her seat, lip-synching, "We got a thing goin' on."*

The collaboration it took to bring Daemine and Natalie's story to NPR damn near drove me—and my long-suffering colleagues—crazy. I'm happiest working alone. Teaching, writing, especially writing. Alone, thank you, alone, the worker who can't work unless an EXIT sign glows somewhere. The grown-up cowgirl singing, "Don't fence me in."

My local producer is a soul sister, my Washington producer at the time, a stubborn genius. Nonetheless, as the Daemine commentary (which had begun to seem like "The dah-dum! Commentary") became increasingly tangled among three women's disparate ages, aesthetics, and, as I saw it, 'hoods, all I wanted to do was quit. Maybe take a job as a buffet hostess, disappear into the reliable cacophony of the slots, resume smoking, get ancient, and write wistful poems for the *Mojave News*.

My relationship with Daemine and Natalie held me fast. I knew my friends not in some electronic void, but in the buzz of casino lounges, Daemine's voice a hot line to the past, Natalie's openness easing my heart. That much I knew, and staying true to it brought weeks of being caught between two producers, doubt, tantrums (mine), and at least one night of no sleep at all.

I restored computer Scrabble, decided I could live fine without NPR. I read and reread "The dah-dum! Commentary" and wondered if I was just a prima donna, the spoiled kid my father had always thought I was. If this was connection, I'd take drifting alone in outer space.

I raged through the days, decided the problem was everybody else's pigheadedness, and then I woke one morning from a dream:

> *NPR had hired Ev and me to write the piece on Daemine. He did the grunt work and I wrote. It had taken months. I was sitting at the computer, putting in the finishing touches. He was standing at my left. A new producer came in and I asked him how much we were getting paid.*
>
> *"Well," he said. "It's short, so I'm giving you, Ev, ten dollars and you, Mary, five."*
>
> *I was furious. "After three weeks of solid work?"*
>
> *He shrugged. I stomped out.*

I came awake grinning. I could feel the sheer joy of stomping out. I remembered having asthma as a kid, lying on the living-room couch, stoned on medication, and putting myself deeper into trance by counting the repetitions of diamonds in the upholstery to escape the rasp of each breath. I remembered learning the joy of leaving a man before he could leave me. And dropping out of graduate statistics because every time I tried to force my mind to memorize formulae that didn't make sense, I went blank and panicked. I called Ev in Wyoming and said, "I've got a problem."

He was quiet.

"I run away."

Next morning I called Cindy. "What do we have to do?" The knot between us untangled instantly. In our next conference call with the DC producer, the commentary fell into place. We decided we needed sound and brought Tim Anderson, a Vegas radio genius, in to record during Daemine's next gig at the Edgewater. I'd meet him there.

Then I'd head west. My youngest son, Matt, had recently come back from six years teaching in Japan. He was living in Los Angeles, working as a waiter, writing screenplays. I was eager to see my child, to meet the man he had become.

I'd felt disconnected from my kids for years. By distance. By my belief that they are entitled to their own lives, and my contrary belief that some of their choices were simply wrong. Disconnection seemed the loving way to be a mom. I found myself taking the safe way through our conversations. E-mail had made that easy.

Looking back, I see that disconnection and love cannot coexist. Unconditional love is an oxymoron for ordinary mortals. Love is sloppy. Love is a pain in the ass.

The weekend of Daemine's next gig arrived. I left Flagstaff in a delicate snowstorm, cruised down the long slope into Seligman, and decided to drive old Route 66. I needed a near-empty two-lane, the winter-bare cottonwoods just before the ghost town of Valentine. I needed the Big Nothing in which the rest of my life could surprise me.

The right rear tire blew out six miles east of Kingman. A young girl in a red beater Celica picked me up after a handful of retiree tourons—my age—zoomed by. She was on her way to her second job at Wal-Mart. She'd had a flat in nearly the same place a week earlier and said she was picking me up because somebody'd done the same thing for her.

I called AAA and was rescued by a sweet Brad Pitt look-alike in a black leather jacket and faded Levi's. He changed the tire and said, "I wouldn't trust that doughnut wheel over the pass. You've got that deluxe AAA, let me haul you to Laughlin."

I rode in front. He was hungry for talk. He told me he loved the earth. "It's a living being," he said, "and so is fire—and learning." As we drove up through the old volcanic pass, he said, "See. Those mountains. I love them. They're big and old and they make total sense."

His words were road words. And the half hour in the front seat of the tow truck, Mojave desert stretching away on all sides, the dark road winding up and over, both of us willing to bare our crazy hearts—that was Road Time.

On Road Time, especially in a beater truck, you go only as fast as the laws of physics allow. If you do that Road Time on the skinny blue lines in the atlas, you will hunt out garages and restaurants and those dirt roads and parking lots in which you might sleep. Sometimes you listen to the tapes crammed into the shoe box on the seat beside you, sometimes to nothing but your heartbeat. You go down dead ends, up switchbacks that lead to nothing but sky. It takes a while. You make mistakes. Sometimes they are fatal. More often they bring you to life.

My AAA Black Knight and I drove into Laughlin just past twilight and said good-bye. I checked into my hotel and went directly to the river. Warm desert air held me. The water was a current of stars and neon. The far shore darkened. A plane rose out of the little airport. I knew the Black Mountains' ragged silhouette by where the stars weren't. I drank casino coffee and thought how much it was like twelve-step meeting coffee, lousy and free.

I sipped my coffee and watched, only a little amazed, as a ribbon of pale green light unfurled along the black water. To this day, I don't know what caused it. But for those moments, birds flew in and out of the light. And I stopped thinking.

Twenty-four hours and eight hundred bucks later, I drove

away. The price seemed reasonable, to be a child, and to feel as though I was part of a chain of gifts and people. Natalie and Daemine, a young sister in a red Celica, the AAA membership my mom had given me long before her death, an angel in a black leather jacket, the old, old river, even my gambling jones were shining links. My love for my son was part of the chain, drawing me farther west and into a full-on love affair with a place I thought I hated. Southern California.

Much of our four days together are my son's story. He talked. I listened. And then we drove and drove and drove to Little Saigon and ate spicy pancakes and pho and salt-and-pepper shrimp. We watched a video of Peter Weir's seventies movie *The Last Wave,* an eerie story of the genocide by condescension of indigenous Australians. Matt and I remembered the first time we had seen it, when I was thirty-eight and he was fifteen, and how, at the end, we had looked at each other in the dark theater, our eyes gleaming, and said, "That's how it is."

He drove me on an old Hollywood street and we watched homeless people packing up their bedrooms, folding cardboard, unpeeling duct tape, drinking coffee out of paper cups, and sharing a cigarette. "That's how it is," he said.

Every evening my son and I walked the beaches. On Zuma we were barefoot, the wet sand alive under my feet. It gave a little, it held my steps. I thought to myself that I could be walking along the firm flank of a giant lover. A lover who welcomed my touch, offered more, carried me toward a horizon that moved up and away from the sun.

On Santa Monica we walked the glowing shoreline, fed gulls, went toward Venice, coming at dusk into the last tatters of the bazaar. I bought a bronze Kali statue no taller than my thumb. My son and I turned back, walked toward the lights of the Santa Monica Pier: the Ferris wheel a rainbow roulette wheel, the roller coaster a snake of stars. I took Kali to the ocean and immersed her. The light was nearly gone. She shimmered. For as long as it took to bathe the tiny goddess in the salt water, I believed absolutely in what I was doing.

I collected sea water at Huntington in a Mexican soft drink bottle I found bobbing in the waves. It was the last evening of the trip. My son and I had bought two boxes of French fries. We stood in the dying light and threw them to the screaming gulls. The tide moved out and I followed it. Waves shimmered toward me. I remembered the world was spinning away from the sun. Another day gone.

No guarantees.

My son drove us back to his studio. We stopped on the way at a Japanese shopping center. I asked him to buy me a tiny clay badger I saw in a shop. "It's called a *tanuki*," he said. The clerk wrapped the ninety-nine-cent creature in tissue paper, put it in a flowered bag, and taped the bag shut with My Little Kitty tape. I watched her young hands move with unconscious grace.

I thought about my son. For three days he and I had talked about everything, but especially his years teaching in Osaka, about Buddhism and the ubiquitous Japanese slot machines called pachinko. He had told me that every purchase you make is wrapped with care, as though what passes between customer and clerk is not just a transaction, but something more like two heartbeats.

I packed up the next morning and set Kali and the *tanuki* on the dashboard next to the plastic head of Sylvester the Cat, which I had found cruelly discarded near an old trailer north of Wendover. Sylvester watched ahead, Kali and the *tanuki* covered our back. We made it out of the city without getting lost.

We were near the ruins of an old pink hotel at Ludlow when I began to be flooded with memories: of light dying along the wild Pacific horizon; of my second-oldest son waking me at midnight in the El Tovar Hotel at Grand Canyon, whispering, "You gotta go outside, Mom. There's full moon on the snow. The canyon looks like it's made of ice cream."

I remembered my daughter walking to the edge of Montezuma's Well, dipping her young woman's hands in the dark water, watching the drops fall like crystal back into the little lake, and how later we walked briskly across the mesa-top, pretending we weren't scared of the monsoon lightning snaking to earth a mile away, and how we reached my truck and collapsed in laughter.

I remembered the gracious warmth of the son I didn't raise, how he and his wife welcomed me into their bright home, how they opened their world out to me, as if it had been him, not me, who had left.

My solitary home lay ahead. I went toward my time alone with no regrets. And still, I thought of my grown-up children and let the tears come.

"I am a lucky woman," I whispered to Sylvester, to Kali and the *tanuki,* to my memories, and the huge bright desert that contained us.

# Spirit Line

■ ■ ■

I am just returned from a small book tour for my essay collection. It always feels that way—that I have *been* returned. I'm grateful. To have been carried home, and for what I learned on the long spirit line of the Road.

In Albuquerque, Ev and I took a seventy-minute I-25 detour of twelve blocks. It was near midnight. We were caravanning and do not have cell phones. It was imperative that we not lose sight of each other's truck. We drove five, three, two miles an hour between eighteen-wheelers. We were in the guts of a world made of chrome and honking and exhaust. There was no escape. I was less than gracious until I considered the eternity so many commuters spend trapped in their cars. And how lucky I am to spend so few.

Two days later we country mice forgot what we had learned about big-city driving and turned onto bypass C-470 five miles south of Denver at four-thirty on a Friday afternoon. It took two hours to drive thirty-four miles. There was no highway construction at that time, no accidents. We drove in ordinary commuter traffic.

I looked at what lay along the highway, a ribbon of identical big-box malls. I studied my neighbors. A few talked on their cells. A few wore headphones. Most simply stared ahead, faces tired, jaws set. I wondered if they drove in this slo-mo stampede every weekday. I wondered how they stood it.

That night I read my essays to a few dozen people at Tattered Cover Bookstore in downtown Denver. The audience seemed to be mostly the usual suspects: young wildlife biologists and botanists, somewhat grizzled Ed Abbey fans (male and female), a handful of dreadlocked kids wearing macramé jewelry, fire-eyed women my age, a blond couple in stone-washed denim and Navajo silver, a few younger women relaxing on Mom's Night Out.

It was a dream audience. My listeners laughed, nodded, and murmured, "Right on." I watched sadness grow in a few faces. Anger.

I paused and asked for questions or reactions. A young woman in a bright red T-shirt raised her hand. "A question has been troubling me for a long time," she said, "long before your reading. I have two small kids. I am terrified for their future. I've been taught that life moves in cycles of expansion and contraction. I see growth exploding. Will there be a contraction? Are the cycles still in place?"

I wanted to comfort her, to say easily, "Yes, we move in cycles, our earth and our huge little species are moved in cycles. It will all come out just fine." But I remembered a moment from the day before and could not. At an off-ramp gas station in Colorado Springs, a furious kid in a pickup truck had squealed out of the lot, his back tires tossing rock like shrapnel. Ev had vice-gripped the door handle of his truck. "I want to go after that kid and beat the shit out of him," he said, then shook his head. "Which makes me him. We are *all* spinning out."

I left the mike on the podium and sat on the edge of the stage.

"I'm deeply afraid," I said, "that the incredible speed at which most of us are moving is carrying us out of the natural spiral. We have exceeded some inner and outer gravitational pull. We are flying out of control."

The young mom's warm face and the sorrow in her eyes made me want to lie. I didn't. "If I knew the answer to your question, I'd be Goddess," I said.

She laughed ruefully. "But, where," she said, "is the hope?"

Before I could answer, her friend stood. She was a woman in her early forties, impeccably groomed, hair cut beautifully, her feet in polished top-of-the-line cowgirl boots. I would have said we were about as far apart as two women can be. And then I saw the pain in her eyes.

Her words came slowly. I had heard them three other times on this trip, once at the Albuquerque reading, once during a radio interview, once between old friends. "My only hope," she said, "is that someday, maybe even soon, our species will be gone." Her mouth twisted. "I have just finished raising teenage children. They are supposed to be the hope for the future. I pray not."

She stayed on her feet. I knew there was more.

"Why not?" I asked.

Her eyes misted. "All they care about," she said, "is what they can see on a television screen or a computer. And what they can buy."

She sat down. The room was silent.

She stood again. "I'm sorry," she said. "I think all I was really saying is that I need, we need, some new kind of hope. I know I've run out."


Recently I sat in a circle with nine teenage writing students and their teacher. I believed I was there to make amends for breaking an earlier date with their class. I told them I'd stood them up for my own writing and to be with a heartsick friend. The kids were, of course, compassionate. A girl thanked me for my honesty. A boy said, "Well, that's cool. Want to hear a poem?"

Another boy read his fantasy about a hero and a Gatekeeper. We talked about writer's block. And then the teacher read a poem his four-and-a-half-year-old daughter, Arin, had written:

> *I ride in my staff*
> *with the holy spirit inside of me.*
> *The stars are beautiful.*
> *And the moon sparkles with joy.*
> *And men have standed on the moon.*
> *"Oh Star, you are my best friend."*
> *I love the moon. It is so beautiful.*

"Your daughter is four and a half?" I said.

The teacher nodded.

"You take her out on walks into the forest and help her write poetry?" I said.

He grinned.

"So," I said, "when you were four and a half, did your dad do that stuff with you?"

"Not hardly," he said.

Most of the kids laughed. With empathy. With irony. Too young, I thought. You are too young to laugh like that.

"I'd like to know," I said, "what you guys were like at four and a half, and how your parents cared for you."

One boy said he had always been treated with unconditional love. All his questions had been answered, and when his parents had no answer, they told him they didn't know. One girl said her mother had always been there for her, no matter what. The sturdy boy said, "My job was to be quiet and stay out of the way. I knew that at four. The TV was my baby-sitter."

Others talked of divorce, of raising themselves, of a drunk dad and foul-mouthed stepmother, of more than one set of parents who clutched a child "like a rope in a tug-of-war."

What comes next I offer as a spirit line for those two Denver mothers, the nine Flagstaff teenage writers and their teacher, to any of you who have just read the words "like a rope in a tug-of-war" and understood:

I sit on my beautiful back porch in beautiful light in beautiful freedom. I sit with Mr. Fear. He has pulled up a lawn chair and he is grinning. If how I feel is what lies under all our busyness, our cocaine and generic beer, our falling in and out of love, falling in and out of the huge blue of the Internet, our sixty-hour work weeks, our eighteen hours at the slots, our fortunes spent on face-lifts and nose jobs and tit jobs so we don't have to get old and discarded and, by virtue of nothing but time and loss, be assigned to the third wheelchair from the left at the Elderlove Care Center—then I know why *nobody* wants to quit *anything*.

Here is medicine:

I take forty-five minutes to wash my dishes. Start to finish. I pick up two empty gallon jugs and walk slowly to the shower house. I am surrounded by delicate light, by the scent of pine. North, the mountains rise against a monsoon sky. Inside me, words rattle: *pick up some wood on the way back in, get the water boiling and finish up that letter to the forest service, you can make phone calls while you're waiting, hurry up, what are you doing about the novel, what are you doing about money, you're lazy, lazy, lazy.* . . .

I stop. I stand in a shaft of sunlight and set the empty jugs down on the pine needles. A small breeze comes up. My face is warm from sun, cool from wind. I realize I am out of breath.

I breathe.

I pick up the jugs and go into the shower house. Bluto the Cat ambles in. Jackie Gleason in a fuzzy tux. He looks down into the drain. He's pretty sure there is a fish in there. I fill the jugs

with hot water. He ducks the splashes, regards me with an accus-
ing eye.

I walk back to the cabin. There seems to be one less chicken
in the chicken yard. I wonder if my landlady will bring me a perfectly barbecued drumstick. I go into my cool cabin and pour
hot water into the teakettle. I light the stove and think how
lucky I am to have propane, to have a stove. To be washing
dishes for one woman. My own.

I carry two empty jugs back to the shower house, where Bluto
is still studying the drain. "Give up, pal," I say. "It's an illusion."
I fill one jug with hot water, one with cold. Bluto gives up. I let
him lead the way. I move at his pace. He looks back over his
shoulder. It's easy to imagine a grin, imagine the Big Guy saying,
"About time you humans caught on."

While the water boils, I unload the dishpan and pile the dirty
dishes in. They are beautiful, the hand-painted cup with the soft
yellow sun in its bottom; the sandwich plate with a Mimbres
bunny; the green and rose and tangerine Fiesta bowls; the brown
and white cup my friend, potter Joann Gentle, stamped with
leaping rabbits she designed. I pour dish soap over everything.

I take the big blue enamel rinse pan to the back porch and
pour gray water on the comfrey and sunflowers. When I come
in, the water is boiling. I shake cleanser into the bottom of the
rinse pan, drop in the dishcloth, and pour boiling water. I pour
more boiling water over the dishes. I have been careful to place
a metal spoon in the crystal glass Kathleen brought me back
from Ireland. I consider the word *pour* and add it to my list of
favorites.

I carry the rinse pan to the shower house. The light grows
brighter. I stop, set the pan on the pine needles, take off my
sweatshirt and drape it over what's left of the woodpile. Sun
touches my bare arms. I raise my face to its warmth, close my
eyes, see pure rose behind my lids.

I continue. The shower house is still in shadow. I scrub out the rinse pan, pour in hot water, empty, pour, empty. I am tempted to have deep thoughts and don't. I half-fill the rinse pan with hot water, lift it carefully, and step out into the light.

I can't carry a full pan because a lumbar disk in my back is not what it once was. I walk slowly, not because of that, but because monsoon clouds have begun to scud in. They whip shadows across the wildflowers I planted in front of my cabin. Fuchsia deepens to madder; bright gold becomes copper. I think that later I will check the evening primrose out back.

No running water. Pure luxury.

I set the rinse pan on the counter just above the sink, add the third jug of hot water, and test the temperature. The water is too hot. I walk out to the dirt road and take my mail from the box. There are too many bills, a dazzling postcard offering me free nights and a fabulous *WELCOME* gift at my favorite casino, and there is a priority package I have been expecting. I hold it carefully in my hands. It is, in many ways, a gift from a lover, and a gift from the past.

Back in the kitchen, I reheat my morning coffee, take the cup to the back porch, sit on the top step, do nothing but sip coffee and watch the monsoon race in—and wait for God to strike me dead. *Lazy. Lazy.*

The first fat drops of rain slam down. I go into the kitchen, test the dishwater and find it perfect. I pick up the sun cup, wash it, place it gently in the rinse pan; follow suit with the Mimbres plate, the Fiestaware, Joann's rabbit mug. I gather a handful of silverware and wash, drop Goodwill forks and my mother's silver into the rinse water. The crystal glass is last. I wash it, dip it in the rinse water, and set it upside down on a red bandanna to dry.

Thunder cracks what's left of morning. The lamp on the refrigerator goes out. I keep washing dishes, put the frying pan and yesterday's rice pan in the soapy water, take Joann's mug out of the rinse water and set it in the drying rack. As always, I feel as though I have just been given a beautiful new mug. It is the same at the Laundromat when I take the clothes from the dryer. New clothes. Abundance. This in a woman for whom a dozen jackpots would never be enough.

This is the woman who once washed her family's clothes in a ghetto Laundromat. Six loads. If you had told her then that she would someday read Raymond Carver's essay "Fires" and understand she had kin, she would not have believed you.

The dish rack is full. The lamp flickers on. I see the colors of the dishes leap up neon: pink, jade, scarlet. I scrub the frying pan, rinse it, and set it on a lit stove burner to dry. I scrub out the rice pan and put it in the rack, and I realize my breathing is steady, my mind clear.

I wipe down the counter, the top of the coffeemaker, the toaster, wring out the soapy cloth and drop it into the rinse water, along with the plastic scrubber. I rinse them, turn off the burner under the dry frying pan, and carry cloth and scrubber to the back line, where I hang them near the prayer flags. The wash water is still too hot to carry to the wildflowers. Besides, they glitter with monsoon.

I take the package I have brought from the mailbox to the back porch, sit and hold it in my lap. The sky has cleared. I wait till raindrops stop falling from the pine branches. The dealer has wrapped the package carefully. I peel tape back. One strip at a time.

When the tape is gone, I open the envelope. The comic book is in a sturdy plastic cover. There is a slip of paper with the dealer's name and a stamp of authenticity. I hold my breath and slide the comic from the acetate. Classics Illustrated. *Arabian Nights.*

The comic book smells of mildew, of time. I open it. It is both less and much more beautiful than I remember. The pictures are no longer luminous, but I see clearly the art in each of them. I find a craft even more wonderful. It has taken fifty-five years to learn to recognize art and craft. And to be faithful as a child to magic.

She is there. Scheherazade. And she is not simply a voice. I turn the page and read her words to her father. She is being taken to the cruel Sultan, a man who marries beautiful women and has them beheaded next morning. Her father is in agony. She smiles. "Worry not, Father. I am too fond of my head. I will find a way to keep it." A few pages later there are jade leaves and garnet berries, and a red crescent moon caught in the branches of a tree whose twisting branches might be serpents. When I turn to the first page to see who the artist is, I read this name: Lillian Chestney. I understand. A woman draws stories to save her life, and in so doing, helps a little girl stay alive—long enough to become a woman, a woman content to have no idea of what comes next.

So be it. Blessed be.

MARY SOJOURNER
FLAGSTAFF, ARIZONA
MARCH 2003

# Gratitude

■ ■ ■

*At dawn, we go to the edge of the mesa*
*to thank our god*
*for another day of life.*
*At sunset, we do the same.*

*—*VIOLET S.

*I thank Our Lady of What Goes Around Comes Around*
*For the many failures of the external in my life,*
*for the breaking of my vows, and the keeping,*
*for the Scheherazades,*
*and our spirit lines spinning out. . . .*

# Acknowledgments

■ ■ ■

Thank you to Sarah McGrath for midwifing this book through a difficult (external and internal) gestation and one of those labors that seem to go on forever. Her patience and wisdom are those of an elder. She taught a woman who thought she knew everything! To my agent, Judith Riven, who was the labor coach who reminded me I could not run away; to the fine, fine editors in my life: Deborah Clow *(Northern Lights)*, Paul Larmer and Betsy Marston *(Writers on the Range)*, Lois Rosenthal (the once and future *Story* magazine), Cindy Carpien, Neva Grant, and Susan Feeney (NPR), Kathleen Walters *(Flagstaff Women's Newsletter)*, Trudy McMurrin, Sandy Crooms, and Margaret Dalrymple (University of Nevada Press); to Susan Stamberg, whose read on *Delicate* was flawless, whose voice launched 2,800 copies; to Carl Lennertz, the bookmaker; to Michael Wolcott, whose penultimate read of the final manuscript was an illumination and whose read on a good nine years of friendship was no less; to Diane Bellock, Barbara Fox, and Roxane George, my sisters on this earth; to Matthew Peterson, my colleague and kin in this work; to Sam and Anna Peterson, for bailing me out with love; to Mary Jae Peterson, for who she is; to Steven Pressfield, whose book *The War of Art* is the only book on writing any writer needs to read; to independent bookstores in America, who carried (in the finest sense of the word) my first short story collection with enthusiasm; and to all my sisters and brothers in the rooms in which bad coffee, corny advice, and lifesaving love are served.

MARY SOJOURNER, sixty-four, began her professional writing at forty-five. Her work includes short stories, essays, a novel, columns for *Writers on the Range,* and commentaries for National Public Radio. She lives in a two-room cabin in Flagstaff, Arizona, with no running water, a woodstove, more than enough solitude, and when she is discouraged, the lyrics to Ani DiFranco's "My IQ" alive in her heart.